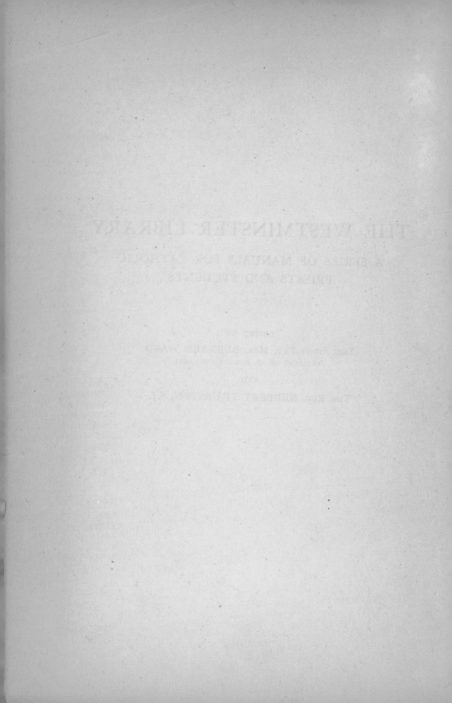

THE WESTMINSTER LIBRARY

A SERIES OF MANUALS FOR CATHOLIC PRIESTS AND STUDENTS

EDITED BY

THE RIGHT REV. MGR. BERNARD WARD
PRESIDENT OF ST. EDMUND'S COLLEGE

AND

THE REV. HERBERT THURSTON, S.J.

THE EARLY CHURCH

IN THE

LIGHT OF THE MONUMENTS

A STUDY IN CHRISTIAN ARCHÆOLOGY

BY

ARTHUR STAPYLTON BARNES, M.A.

UNIVERSITY COLLEGE, OXFORD, TRINITY COLLEGE, CAMBRIDGE
CHAMBERLAIN OF HONOUR TO H.H. PIUS X.
CORRESPONDING MEMBER OF THE SOCIETÉ ARCHÉOLOGIQUE DE FRANCE
AND OF THE ARCADIA OF ROME

WITH ILLUSTRATIONS

LONGMANS, GREEN AND CO.

39 PATERNOSTER ROW, LONDON
NEW YORK, BOMBAY AND CALCUTTA

1913

EDITORS' PREFACE.

THIS series of Handbooks is designed to meet
a need, which, the Editors believe, has been
widely felt, and which results in great measure
from the predominant importance attached to
Dogmatic and Moral Theology in the studies
preliminary to the Priesthood. That the first
place must of necessity be given to these
subjects will not be disputed. But there remains a large outlying field of professional
knowledge which is always in danger of being
crowded out in the years before ordination, and
the practical utility of which may not be fully
realised until some experience of the ministry
has been gained. It will be the aim of the
present series to offer the sort of help which is
dictated by such experience, and its developments will be largely guided by the suggestions,
past and future, of the Clergy themselves. To
provide Textbooks for Dogmatic Treatises is
not contemplated—at any rate not at the outset.
On the other hand, the pastoral work of the
missionary priest will be kept constantly in
view, and the series will also deal with those
historical and liturgical aspects of Catholic

belief and practice which are every day being brought more into prominence.

That the needs of English-speaking countries are, in these respects, exceptional, must be manifest to all. In point of treatment it seems desirable that the volumes should be popular rather than scholastic, but the Editors hope that by the selection of writers, fully competent in their special subjects, the information given may always be accurate and abreast of modern research.

The kind approval of this scheme by His Grace the Archbishop of Westminster, in whose Diocese these manuals are edited, has suggested that the series should be introduced to the public under the general title of THE WEST-MINSTER LIBRARY. It is hoped, however, that contributors may also be found among the distinguished Clergy of Ireland and America, and that the Westminster Library will be representative of Catholic scholarship in all English-speaking countries.

CONTENTS.

vii

PART III.

THE DEVELOPMENT OF CHURCH BUILDINGS.

LIST OF ILLUSTRATIONS

ix

INTRODUCTORY CHAPTER.

ON THE STUDY OF ARCHÆOLOGY.

ARCHÆOLOGY has for its domain the study of ancient monuments in the light of history and with the object of assisting historical knowledge. There cannot be, therefore, any real and essential distinction between the two sciences. It makes no difference whether our knowledge of the past is drawn from parchments or papyri covered with characters written by the hand of some ancient scribe, or from stones or medals engraved with monumental inscriptions and bearing pictorial representations of historical events. Both alike, the written manuscript and the pictured stone, are sources of history, while the stone has the added advantage that it is not liable to alteration or even falsification at the hands of an ignorant or a fraudulent copyist.

The function of the archæologist is, then, to prepare the material for the historian. He has a vast field before him, to a great extent even now left unexplored, which it is his duty to investigate and to survey. There are thousands upon thousands of objects ready for him, the rich heritage which the past has handed down, and it is his duty to sort these out into their due divisions, to compare one with another, and so to make them tell their stories, and add each its little piece to the great work of the reconstruction of the past. For the historian cannot do without this assistance if he is to give a true picture of the period with which he is dealing. Manuscripts and written material are often quite inadequate to establish facts which are yet of the first importance for any real understanding of the politics and thought of the past.

Let us take a concrete instance. History, to use the word in the sense of written records, is able to give us only the most inadequate information on the subject of the political economies of the Roman Empire. It is from the study of numismatics that we are made aware of the perilous state to which the finances of the Empire were reduced through almost the whole of the third century, when a debased coinage of scarcely any intrinsic value, put forth in immense quantities, took the place for commercial purposes of the sound money of silver and gold which had hitherto been in use. The position, in fact, was identical with that which we have seen in more modern times, when some state whose financial position has been insecure has tried to bolster up its falling credit by the forced issue of a paper currency which is not convertible to real value. The usual inevitable consequences immediately followed. We can at once explain the enormous taxation and the constant vexatious acts of legislation which were the means of involving the municipal governments in hopeless debt, and in the end were no small factor in bringing about the dissolution of the imperial power. The barbarians indeed gave the final blow which brought down the tottering Empire to its knees, but the Empire would never have been in danger from the attacks of such a foe, were it not that it was already weakened by the loss of power which followed as a disastrous but inevitable consequence from a policy financially and commercially rotten.[1]

Other similar instances in which history, unassisted by archæology, would be unable to give a true picture of past events, will readily occur to the mind of every

---

[1] I owe this illustration, as well as others in this chapter, to the late Commendatore Stevenson.

COIN OF BRUTUS

LABARUM OF CONSTANTINE

COIN OF BRUTUS
(reverse)

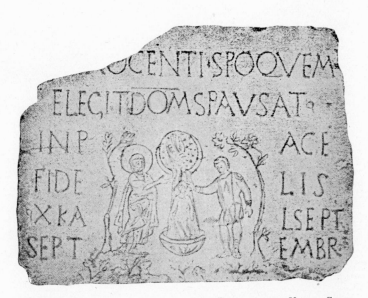

INSCRIPTION AT AQUILEIA, SHOWING THE BAPTISM OF A YOUNG GIRL

From Marucchi's " Eléments d'Archéologie" (Desclée, De Brouwer et Cie)

student.   The impression formed by the study of the records of history on the subject of the assassination of Cæsar may well be that Brutus was indeed, as partisans of the French Revolution loved to represent him, a true patriot, who sacrificed his friend to the dictates of his conscience, and would allow no human affection to stand in the way of what he saw to be his duty.   But when one has once seen the famous medal of the Ides of March, a medal which bears the effigy of Brutus himself stamped on its surface, one cannot help realising that it was personal spite and envy against Cæsar himself, and not against the monarchical principle, which was the motive which led to the assassination.   For in the Roman State to place one's likeness on the public money was precisely to claim, in the most formal manner possible, sovereign power and dominion over all.   That was the very point, it will be remembered, of our Saviour's argument, when He bade them bring Him the coin in which the tribute had to be paid, and argued from the head of Tiberius stamped upon it, that it was the duty of a subject to pay to his sovereign the tribute that was levied upon him.   The use of money bearing Cæsar's effigy implied the acceptance of Cæsar's authority.   No other Roman at the time of Cæsar's assassination, but only the great Julius himself, had ever in his own lifetime seen his own head stamped upon a coin.   How then, if Brutus had his own effigy stamped upon the coinage, could he possibly have been a genuine opponent of the principle of kingship and of the concentration of all authority in the hands of a single individual?   One feels, as one looks at this most important piece of evidence, that there is something at least to be said for the vehemence of Dante, who, far from extolling Brutus as a lofty patriot, puts him along with Judas Iscariot in the lowest depths of hell, as one who betrayed his sovereign and did his best, for selfish motives, to ruin and destroy the country to which he owed allegiance and faithful service.

That Brutus was himself responsible for the issue of the coin, and that it was not merely the rash act of some unwise admirer, is shown by the words of Dion Cassius. " On the coins which he caused to be struck he exhibited a likeness of himself, and a cap and two daggers ; intimating by this design and by the legend that, conjointly with Cassius, he had restored his country to liberty." [1]   The inscription EID. MAR. declares the fatal day, the Ides of March, on which the bloody deed was done.

These illustrations are taken from secular history, but it would be easy to give others in closer connection with the domain of Christian Archæology.   Where could we find, for instance, so convincing a testimony to the Catholic faith and practice of the Christians of Phrygia in the second century as is afforded by the discovery of the Stele of Abercius, to which frequent appeal is made in succeeding chapters.   Or, again, how much valuable light is thrown upon the position at Rome and in the Empire after the changes wrought by the Edict of Milan, and upon the character and beliefs of Constantine himself, by a careful study of the coinage issued both at Rome and Constantinople during the twenty-five years of that Emperor's reign. " He was at best only half Pagan, half Christian, who could seek to combine the worship of Christ with the worship of Apollo, having the name of one with the figure of the other impressed upon his coins, and ordaining the observance of Sunday under the name of *Dies Solis* in his celebrated decree of March, 321." [2] It is easy to exaggerate the force of such evidence, but the least that it can be said to demonstrate is that the Emperor was keenly alive to the value of compromise,

[1] Dion Cassius, xlvii. 25.   [2] *Encycl. Brit.* art. Constantine.

and, while by no means indifferent to the vital truths of Christianity, eager to go as far as possible in the direction of propitiating the adherents of the older religion.

These are instances of the help given to the historian by the study of isolated objects of antiquity, like monuments or coins.   But it is often the case that conclusions of the greatest importance can be drawn from whole series of facts considered in their mutual bearing on one another.   It is often asserted, for instance, that the Christian community of Rome in the age of persecution was neither large nor wealthy. The reader will have grounds laid before him in a later chapter from which he will be able to judge for himself how entirely opposite to the real fact such assertions actually are.   But, without going any farther for proof, we can settle the question for ourselves by a mere inspection of a map of the country immediately round the city of Rome.   Note the tracks of the ancient roads which ran in every direction from the gates of the city into the surrounding country.   Land on the sides of those roads must inevitably, from the advantage of its accessibility, have commanded the highest prices in ancient times.   Of all these roads the *Via Appia*, leading out to the Alban Hills, was by common consent the mistress and the Queen.   Land immediately abutting on that great thoroughfare must have been the most costly of all in the neighbourhood of Rome.   Yet we find that the cemeteries of the Church, and especially that great burial ground which was the official property of the Church as such, the Cemetery of St. Callixtus, were constructed under the very best of the land which occupied this specially favoured position.   Since these Catacombs are wholly excavated under the surface of land which was private property, so much so that to this day we can trace out the boundaries of the various properties by simply

noting where the galleries come to an end, it follows
necessarily that vast quantities of this most valuable
land was in the hands of Christian owners.   No
poverty-stricken body of uneducated slaves, such as
some are fond of imagining the early Roman Christians to have been, could possibly have owned land in
such a district, or, owning it, would have dedicated it
to a use which, by taking away the possibility of
selling it, inevitably destroyed its value in the open
market.   The hills on the right and the left of this
great thoroughfare, right up to the second milestone,
with the exception only of a few limited strips, are all
honeycombed beneath with galleries and given over
to the final disposition of the bodies of the faithful.
When we reflect on the enormous value of landed
property in a district so much sought after, does it
not open out before us a new and unexpected vision
of the power and the riches of the Christian community even before the persecutions came to an end ?

If we turn to the *Via Salaria*, another road of almost equal importance, the case is even more striking.
A fairly large district along the *Via Appia* lies low and
is unsuitable for the purposes of burial in Catacombs.
But the *Via Salaria* runs almost wholly on high
ground, and here the whole soil is undermined by
Christian galleries.   The Christians, then, even before
Constantine, were in possession of the best lands near
Rome, on the borders of the main roads which gave
access to the city.   Wherever we turn we find the
same story.   The whole city seems to have been surrounded with similar *hypogea*, the last resting-places
of primitive Christians.   So vast a property in land
in the most favoured spots in close proximity to the
city, can scarcely have any other meaning than that
all Rome was surrounded by Christian estates, covered,
no doubt, with splendid villas and beautiful gardens,
the property of the noble classes of Roman citizens.

We begin to understand that had not Christianity been a religion which preached humility and inculcated submission to existing powers, Christians might have possessed themselves of supreme authority in the city a long while before the Edict of Milan.   The peace of Constantine was not so much an unexpected boon, as a necessity forced on by the political needs of the moment.   No other choice was possible at the beginning of the fourth century except that between civil war if Christianity was to be destroyed, and the attainment of peace by permitting to Christians a legal and unmolested existence.   Even if Constantine had not been drawn to the latter alternative by his sincere admiration for Christians and his belief in the religion they professed, he would have been driven sooner or later to grant the boon because of the numbers and importance to which the Christians had attained in the very capital of the Empire, and of the world.   And all this we should know for certain, even if every historical document of the period had perished, from the mere study of the extent and position of the Catacombs which encircle Rome.

The field of research which is open to a student of Archæology, since it includes the whole study of the remains of past ages, is so vast that he will be well advised, if he desires to attain to any kind of eminence, to limit himself strictly to a single branch.   Even Christian Archæology, strictly so-called, is too extended a study to allow of any detailed knowledge of all its many sub-divisions by any one who is unable to give up his whole life to this single object.   Even here some definite limits must be placed by most students to the extent of their interests and their aims.   It is better, for instance, to be a real authority on numismatics or on palæography than to try to cover a much wider field with less accuracy and real knowledge.   Such studies as those of Mgr. Wilpert on the pictures of the Catacombs, or of M. Muntz on the Mosaics of Rome, far exceed in value the labours of hundreds of less specialised workers. At the same time it is not possible to do good work in any one department without at least a general knowledge of the whole field.

A student who is beginning a new subject like that of Archæology will do well in the first place to read a generalised sketch which covers a wide area, and consists of conclusions rather than of facts. At this early stage of his knowledge, he will be apt to be confused by too large a number of facts and details, and to fail in consequence to obtain any clear ideas of what the facts point to. He will find himself, in effect, in the position of the countryman of the story, who complained when they brought him up to visit the capital that he was wholly unable to see the town because it was always hidden by the houses. His knowledge will very likely be accurate and extensive enough, but he will be unable to make proper use of it because his view will be circumscribed and limited by his want of any clear conception of the greater whole which lies beneath and beyond the immediate series of facts of which he has obtained cognisance.

Such a general sketch it has been the object of this book to supply. It is intended to arouse interest and to lead on to further and deeper study, the materials for which will be found indicated in the Bibliographical notes at the end of the volume.

The author's thanks are especially due to his friend, Prof. Marucchi, for his kind interest, and for permission to reproduce many illustrations from his monumental work on the Lateran Museum. He would also thank others who have given similar permissions which are acknowledged on the various plates.

PART I.

CHAPTER I.

The Apostles at Rome.

IN the sixteenth century and for some time afterwards it came to be the fashion among Protestant controversialists, while they were ready enough to acknowledge the truth of the story which told how St. Paul had preached and died in Rome, to deny that the same was also true of St. Peter. Such a position was rendered possible by the paucity of the literary evidence available. In the New Testament itself it is admitted that no clear and undoubted proof of the fact is to be found, and to those whose watchword of religion was "the Bible and the Bible only," this seemed, no doubt, a strong and almost irrefragable argument. But, at any rate in dealing with historical facts, there can be no possible reason for confining ourselves to the evidence contained in Holy Scripture ; and once we look outside its covers, we find that evidence exists in plenty. No other place than Rome ever claimed to be the scene of St. Peter's last labours and of his martyrdom, and when we realize how absolutely unanimous all antiquity is upon this point, the wonder comes to be that any scholars should have been found " so hardily sceptical," as Bishop Ellicott of Gloucester phrased it, as to deny a fact based upon evidence " as

strong, early, and wide as that on which we believe
that Hannibal invaded Italy".

But another and quite independent line of evidence
is open to us, which has hitherto, in England at least,
been very generally neglected. It is that which is
drawn from the study of archæology, and is admirably summed up by Prof. Lanciani in his excellent
book on "Pagan and Christian Rome". " I write," he
says, "about the monuments of Rome from a strictly
archæological point of view, avoiding questions which
pertain, or are supposed to pertain, to religious controversy. For the archæologist the presence and
execution of SS. Peter and Paul in Rome are facts
established beyond the shadow of a doubt by purely
monumental evidence. . . . There is no event of the
imperial age, and of imperial Rome, which is attested
by so many noble structures, all of which point to the
same conclusion—the presence and execution of the
Apostles within the capital of the empire. When
Constantine raised the monumental basilicas over their
tombs on the Via Cornelia and the Via Ostiensis;
when Eudoxia built the church ad Vincula; when
Damasus put a memorial tablet in the Platonia ad
Catacumbas; when the houses of Pudens and Aquila
were turned into Christian oratories; when the name
of Nymphae Sancti Petri was given to the springs of
the Catacombs of the Via Nomentana; when Christians
and pagans alike named their children Peter and Paul;
when the twenty-ninth day of June was accepted as
the anniversary of St. Peter's execution; when sculp-
tors, painters, medallists, goldsmiths, workers in glass
and enamel, and engravers of precious stones, all
began to reproduce in Rome the likenesses of the
Apostles at the beginning of the second century and
continued to do so until the fall of the empire; must
we consider them all as labouring under a delusion or

as conspiring in the commission of a gigantic fraud?
Why were such proceedings accepted without protest
from whatever city, from whatever community, if there
were any other which claimed to own the genuine
tombs of St. Peter and St. Paul?"[1]

The Places of Martyrdom.

This monumental evidence, the special domain of
Christian archæology, thus briefly and vividly sketched
out by Prof. Lanciani, it is the object of the present
chapter to draw out in rather greater detail. We
begin with the spots in Rome connected by tradition
with the two Apostles.

Not all the churches in Rome which assert such
claims are altogether worthy of acceptance. Especially
must we mention in this category the well-known
church upon the Janiculum, which claims to be the
scene of St. Peter's passion. Its history goes back only
to the fourteenth century, and was the outcome of faulty
antiquarianism and of wrong deductions from the records
of the past. The real place of the martyrdom was,
there can be no doubt, the *spina* of the Circus of Nero,
close to the obelisk in the centre, and, therefore, just
outside the eastern transept of the present basilica.
The ancient authorities are in complete agreement.
The "Liber Pontificalis"[2] tells us that the grave was
near to the place of martyrdom; the "Martyrium B.
Petri Ap."[3] tells us that it was close to the obelisk;
and, lastly, the "Acta Petri"[4] adds the detail that it
was on the *spina* of the Circus *intra duas metas*. Now
the ancient place of the obelisk, before it was moved
to the centre of the *piazza* by Sixtus V, may be dis-

[1] Lanciani, "Pagan and Christian Rome," p. 125.
[2] "Lib. Pont.," i. p. 64, ed. Duchesne.
[3] "Acta Petri," ed. Lipsius, p. 13.   [4] *Ibid.* p. 216.

covered by a flat stone with an inscription let into the pavement, close by the door of the present sacristy, and this enables us to locate the exact spot of the martyrdom with considerable accuracy.

St. Paul, who as a Roman citizen was beheaded, was taken to the third milestone on a small road branching from the Via Ostiensis. The place is now known as the Three Fountains, but was then called the *Aquae Salviae*. No other place has ever claimed the honour of being the scene of his martyrdom, and there is no reason whatever for doubting the truth of the tradition.[1]

The Tombs on the Vatican and the Via Ostiensis.

No other monuments of apostolic Rome can make so absolute a claim to authenticity as the two tombs which are now covered respectively by the great basilicas of St. Peter and St. Paul. Already at the beginning of the second century we have notice of their existence in the words of the priest Caius, "I can show you," he says, "the monuments (*tropaea*) of the Apostles, for you will find them on the Vatican and on the Ostian Way";[2] and Eusebius himself, who has preserved this testimony, bears witness that in his time the monuments were still extant.

Each of these two primitive apostolic sepulchres was necessarily situated outside the city limits, for burial within those limits was not allowed, and they are each of them placed as near as might be to the spot of the actual martyrdom. As regards the tomb of St. Peter there can be no doubt that the place was used for burials in the age of Nero, for many tombs of that period were discovered in the course of the excavations made when the basilica was rebuilt. A small

---

[1] See " Bull. d' arch. crist.," 1869, p. 83.
[2] Eus., " H.E.," ii. p. 25.

portion of ground in this area was already in Christian
hands, even before St. Peter's death, and it was here
that the remains of the martyrs in the great persecution
of A.D. 64 had been deposited. More than 1600 years
afterwards, when the excavations were being made for
the great *baldacchino* over the tomb, these remains
were discovered close to the tomb of the Apostle himself. He was laid, therefore, as that discovery clearly
proved, in ground that was already Christian, and
already rendered holy in Christian eyes by being the
resting-place of so many who had given their lives for
the faith.[1]

The body of St. Paul is said in like manner to have
been buried by a matron called Lucina in her own
ground on the Ostian Way, a little beyond the first
milestone.

In neither case were the Apostles laid in one of those
subterranean cemeteries which we know by the name
of the Catacombs. The time for these had not yet
come. Each of these two apostolic tombs was on the
surface of the ground, in vaults dug down near the
road, and approached by a staircase on that side.
Similar graves of the same period may still be seen
on the Via Appia and Via Latina.

In the case of St. Peter's tomb, but not in that of
St. Paul, an addition was made later on to this primitive vault. An upper chamber was added before the
end of the first century by Pope St. Anacletus.[2] The
building, although to some extent it still exists, is
hidden from our eyes by the decorations of the High
Altar at St. Peter's. For a moment, however, it was
uncovered, during the excavations of 1626, and although the excavators did not altogether realize what
it was that they had found, a description of it has been

[1] Barnes, "St. Peter in Rome," pp. 91, 331.
[2] "Lib. Pont.," i. p. 125, ed. Duchesne.

left on record by one of their number. It had the appearance to his eyes of a small heathen temple, and was covered, as to its upper part only (which showed that the greater part of the fabric had always been underground), with ornamental work in stucco.[1]

Round this *memoria* of St. Peter were buried, surrounding him like bishops at a synod, the first twelve of his successors. Their bodies were found in 1626, "clothed with long robes down to the heels, dark and almost black with age, and swathed with bandages like infants ; the bandages passing also over the head".[2] All crumbled into dust as soon as the air reached them.

In this state the tombs remained till the peace of the Church, and then Constantine caused the great basilicas to be built above them. But before we come to that date we have to speak of a translation of the relics of each of these two Apostles which was rendered necessary by the edict of 258, an edict which deprived the Christian body of the protection which had till then been enjoyed by its graves and monuments. For the first time the relics of the Apostles were in real danger of profanation.

The Platonia ad Catacumbas.

There is a good deal of confusion about the translation of the relics which took place at this time, and yet as to the reality of the fact there can be no doubt whatever. The greater part of the confusion seems to have resulted from a projection backwards of the story, which really belongs to 258, to the original time of the burial of the Apostles. Consequently the opinion grew up that there were really two separate occasions on which the bodies had been taken to the Catacombs

[1] Barnes, " St. Peter at Rome," pp. 334, 340.
[2] *Ibid.* p. 323.

at S. Sebastiano. There is a long literature on the point, and there is no object in our going into the question now. The only point we need dwell upon, one which is more or less historically certain, is the fact of the translation and hiding of the relics, to save them from possible danger of profanation, in the year 258.

In an ancient manuscript, which contains a Hieronynian Martyrology and is preserved at Berne, we read :—

III. Kal Julias.

> Romæ Via Aurelia S.S. Apostolorum Petri et Pauli—Petri in Vaticano, Pauli vero in Via Ostiensi, utrumque in Catacumbis, passi sub Nerone, Basso et Tusco consulibus.

That is to say, that on the 29th June there were three feasts kept at Rome : of St. Peter on the Vatican, of St. Paul on the Ostian Way, and of both at the Catacombs. The consular date, which is A.D. 258, cannot be connected with the martyrdoms, since both suffered under Nero, but must have to do with the third locality mentioned, that of the Catacombs.

The probable solution is the one we have already mentioned. In the year 258 the right to a quiet possession of the cemeteries was taken away from the Christians. All those cemeteries at any rate which were in the possession of the Church herself became State property ; and among these would be included the tombs of St. Peter and St. Paul. Hence the relics were taken away by night and hidden in another cemetery, that which we now know as S. Sebastiano. Here they were comparatively safe, for not only would the persecutors, even if they wished to desecrate them, have had no clue where they might be hidden, but they would also be protected by the right of private property, since this particular cemetery had not yet passed into the hands of the Church as such, but was still, before the law, the property of a private individual.

The hiding-place in which the bodies were laid may yet be seen. It is under the altar in the crypt which is called the Platonia, and is a square chamber measuring about 8 feet each way, and covered with barrel vaulting, the highest part of which is 8 feet 3 inches from the floor. The vaulting is of later date than the tomb. The floor is composed of two slabs of marble, separated the one from the other by a third slab set vertically, thus forming a large double tomb in which the sarcophagi of the Apostles could be laid side by side.

Whether or not the relics of the Saints would have been in real danger had they remained in their original resting-places we cannot tell. It would have been unlike Romans to make war on the remains of the dead long after the event. In any case, they were safe at S. Sebastiano, and there they remained until the persecution was passed and it was safe to bring them back again to their own proper tombs. The local tradition says that they remained at the Catacombs for forty years, but such periods always tend to grow, and it seems more likely that the period given in the apocryphal Acts in connexion with an imaginary earlier translation has preserved the truth as to the real one, and that they were brought back after a year and seven months, when Gallienus gave back the cemeteries to the Church. But, in any case, the ancient testimonies are much confused, and it is very difficult to get at the real truth of the facts.

The Chair of St. Peter.

Two feasts of the Church, on 18 January and 22 February respectively, are celebrated in com-

memoration of the Chair of St. Peter. By a mis-
understanding of comparatively late date the second
of these feasts has come to be regarded as his Chair
at Antioch, but originally each of the two had reference to Rome, and commemorated two different chairs
or localities in which he sat as bishop and ruled the
Church.

It is recorded in the Acts of Pope Liberius that on
one occasion, being driven from the Lateran and unable to administer baptism at Easter in his own
cathedral, he followed the advice of his deacon, St.
Damasus, and betook himself for the purpose to a
spot close to the Cœmeterium Ostrianum on the Via
Nomentana, because that was the place where St. Peter
had been in the habit of baptizing. Formerly a
baptistery underground in the Cœmeterium Ostrianum
was identified by De Rossi as the scene of this action,
but it is now generally admitted that this identification
cannot be sustained, but that the true spot must have
been somewhere above ground on the Via Salaria,
in an oratory connected with the Villa of the Acilii
Glabriones. There is now no trace of an oratory in
this spot, but the foundations of the villa can still be
seen.

The whole matter is still far from having received
its final solution, but we may state the present opinion
of those who are best qualified to judge, somewhat as
follows :—

St. Peter came first to Rome in the year 42. For
seven years he remained in Rome, not, however, in the
city itself, but rather outside of it in the Villa of the
Acilii, and here he exercised his ministry, baptizing
and preaching. This first coming to Rome, and stay
of seven years, are commemorated on the feast of
18 January. The seven years' stay was terminated by
a decree of Claudius ordering all Jews to leave Rome,

and in consequence St. Peter went away and remained
away for a prolonged period.   When he returned again
to the city, some years afterwards, he did not go back
to his old quarters on the Via Salaria, but took up his
abode within the city itself.   It is this second coming
and abode in Rome which is commemorated by the
feast of 22 February.   His stay during this second
period connects itself especially with two spots, those
which are now known as the two churches of Sta
Prisca and Sta Pudenziana, and which we shall consider
immediately.   It has also a yet more definite memorial
in the actual wooden chair which is still preserved at
St. Peter's and venerated as the chair of the Apostle,
and to this we must now give our attention.

It was placed in the Vatican Basilica, by Pope
St. Damasus, about the year 375.   From that time onwards its history is clear enough.   At an earlier date
we have several references to an actual chair preserved
at Rome, which can scarcely refer to any other than
this.   Thus the third-century poem " Adversus Marcio-
nem" (Migne, "P.L." ii. 1099) mentions a *cathedra
Petrus qua sederat ipse*, a chair on which Peter himself
had sat.   St. Cyprian also speaks of the *gradus cathe-
drae sacerdotalis*, and Tertullian tells his readers to visit
the various churches founded by Apostles in which,
he says, " the very chairs of the Apostles still preside
in their places ".   The history of the chair is, therefore,
well authenticated.

The actual chair is of oak, a perfectly plain arm-
chair with four legs connected with cross-bars.   The
wood is much worm-eaten, and pieces have been cut
from various parts, obviously for relics.   The seat is
1 foot 10 inches above the ground, and it is about
3 feet wide.   There are four iron rings, intended
for carrying-poles, set into the legs.   At a later date,
probably in the ninth century, decorations of acacia

wood with ivories let in have been added to the original chair. The ivories are engraved with the labour of Hercules, not a very appropriate subject. The back is divided by small columns and arches and is open, with a triangular top of similar character. There is hardly enough of the old chair left to enable us to speak very clearly as to its character, but in any case it is quite certain that the idea that it was the

CHAIR OF ST. PETER.

sella curulis or senatorial chair of Pudens, an idea first put forth by Fabeo in the seventeenth century, cannot possibly be sustained. It was of much too plain and simple a character for such an origin to be possible. But there is no reason to doubt the genuineness of the tradition which connects it with the Apostle, and in any case it is one of the most ancient and venerable of all Christian monuments.

Churches and Cemeteries of Apostolic Date.

The tradition of the Church is, as we have said, that St. Peter came first to Rome in the year 42, twenty-five years before his martyrdom in 67. There are, however, few, if any, antiquaries or historians who would be inclined to support the theory that his residence at Rome between these dates was in any way continuous. On the contrary, the general belief is that he was obliged to quit Rome in 49—when Claudius ordered all the Jews to depart from the city. We know of this expulsion from Suetonius, from whom we have also the hint that religious difficulties caused by the Christian propaganda were the cause of the decree, *Judaeos impulsore Chresto assidue tumultuantes Roma expulit* (Suet. " in Claudio," 25). We know of it also from the Acts of the Apostles, where we are told (XVIII. 2) that Aquila and Priscilla had been obliged in consequence to leave Rome, and had come to Ephesus. They did not, however, remain very long away from Rome, for when St. Paul wrote the Epistle to the Romans he sent special salutations to them at Rome. "Salute Prisca and Aquila, my helpers in Christ Jesus, and the church that is in their house" (Rom. XVI. 3).

This little domestic oratory thus mentioned by St. Paul, as already existing by A.D. 58, seems to have grown into the *titulus* or parish church we now know by the name of S. Prisca on the Aventine, which is thus shown to be perhaps the most ancient of all the churches of the city, so far as its origin is concerned.

With it was always in close relation another church on the Viminal, also reputed to be of apostolic date, which we now know by the name of Sta Pudenziana, and which is the titular church of Cardinal Bourne.

There is a good deal which is legendary about the history of these two churches, and it is not always easy to separate the true from the false. With regard to Sta Pudenziana we have a variety of apocryphal, but still extremely ancient, documents whose evidence must be taken with considerable caution. Such are the letter from Pius I to Justin of Vienna, the narratives of Pastor and of Timothy, and, perhaps, the statements of the " Liber Pontificalis ". From them we learn that the church which is now known as Sta Pudenziana was originally the house of Pudens, who was baptized by the Apostles ; that the Apostle St. Peter dwelt there with his convert ; that at first the faithful had their meeting-place in the actual house, but that, later on, Pudenziana, Prassede, and Timothy, the children of Pudens, caused the adjoining baths of Novatus, their brother, to be made into a church by St. Pius I. There is no impossibility in this if we allow the change into a church to have been made when these persons were already advanced in life, and the whole is corroborated by a good deal of independent and undoubtedly genuine evidence. There is no doubt that the church in the fourth century bore the name of *ecclesia Pudentiana*, which would certainly seem to denote a *titulus* erected on the property of the family of Pudens, and not simply a church bearing the name of an individual saint. So, again, the story of the baths of Novatus is confirmed by the evidence of St. Justin Martyr, and by an inscription in the galleries of the Vatican. When excavations were made in 1895 beneath the church, five large halls were discovered, ornamented with pilasters and arches and communicating with one another. There were also two mosaic pavements.   In these remains it was generally agreed that we had recovered the traces of the baths of Novatus, and it is quite possible that when the finances allow of the excavations being carried further, there may be more discoveries which will throw yet further light on the origin of the Church at Rome.

Both these two churches of Sta Pudenziana and Sta Prisca had special relations with the very ancient cemetery on the Via Salaria which is called the cemetery of Priscilla. It seems likely, from inscriptions which have been found in this cemetery, that the ground originally belonged to one Priscilla, who was the wife of one of the Acilii Glabriones, whose villa lay just above. This lady having become a Christian, instituted a cemetery to provide Christian burial in the grounds of her own house. Her namesake, the wife of Aquila, was connected somehow with her, perhaps as a freedwoman of the family ; and this accounts for the connexion to some extent. This cemetery of Priscilla is perhaps the oldest of all the cemeteries of Rome, though not the only one which existed in apostolic times. The others of the same period will be those of Domitilla, the so-called crypts of Lucina in the cemetery of St. Callistus, and another small cemetery, still unexplored, on the Via Aurelia, where SS. Processus and Martinianus, the gaolers of St. Peter, were buried. All these in some degree have apostolic memories, mostly connected with St. Peter, for it is a singular and noteworthy fact that the stay of St. Paul in Rome has left very few traces behind ; far less than is the case with his brother Apostle. The claims of the oratory under the church of Sta Maria in Via Lata cannot be sustained, and the so-called "school of St. Paul," called *alla Regola*, has even less right to serious attention. There is, however, one spot, the so-called Mamertine Prison, which is worthy of more careful examination.

The Mamertine Prison or Tullianum.

This celebrated prison, close to the Capitol, is venerated as having been the spot where the two Apostles were united together in bonds just before their martyrdom, and where St. Peter baptized his gaolers by the aid of a spring which miraculously burst forth in the floor of the dungeon. There is no impossibility in the story, for there is no doubt that the place was used as a prison in imperial times, but the evidence available is not very early. Still we have notices of it as early as the fifth or sixth century in the "Acts" of SS. Processus and Martinianus. In the eighth century we have the pilgrim of Einsiedeln, who speaks of

Fons Sancti Petri ubi est carcer ejus,

so that there can be no question that by that date there was already an oratory on the spot. It would seem, therefore, that the tradition is worthy of all respect, and certainly all would regret it if the belief had to be given up. In the time of the Apostles the staircase which now gives access to the lower prison was not in existence. At that time the only connection of this awful spot with the outer world was by means of a round hole in the centre of the vaulting through which prisoners were lowered.

Other and Doubtful Traditions.

The other spots in Rome which claim to connect themselves with the Apostles cannot be said to have proved their case, though this does not at all necessarily

mean that they are all to be rejected.   The little oratory
of the *Quo Vadis*, for instance, serves to remind us of
a very beautiful story, but it has not much real claim
to authenticity, and the same must be said of the
little chapel on the Ostian Way, which is called the
Oratory of the Separation of the Apostles.   The testimony available for these spots is not very ancient,
but, of course, there is no impossibility that they do
preserve the memory of real occurrences of some
kind.   The church on the Janiculum has no solid
claim at all, but owes its origin to the misunderstand-
ing of ancient documents.   There remain just two
more relics of real importance, and with them our
recapitulation of the memories of the Apostles at Rome
must come to a close.

The Wooden Altar of St. Peter.

The present discipline of the Catholic Church is, as
is well known, that all altars must be of stone.   This
rule knows one exception and only one, and that in
the mother of all churches, the Lateran basilica itself.
Here a small table of wood, which had been carefully
preserved during the ages of persecution, and which
was believed to have been used as an altar by St.
Peter himself, was enclosed in the larger altar of stone,
and forms the actual *mensa* on which the Holy
Sacrifice is now offered.   There can be no doubt that
its authenticity was believed to be beyond question
in 325, when the Lateran became the Cathedral
of Rome.   Otherwise, since the feeling in favour of
stone altars was so strong as to lead to the prohibition of all others, an altar of wood would never have
been allowed to remain as the high altar of the Cathedral Church of Rome.   But we know no details as to
its earlier history.   It is of cedar wood, and apparently

of the same material as the piece preserved at Sta
Pudenziana, which is said to have been left there
when the main portion was removed to the Lateran.

St. Peter's Chains.

The present church of San Pietro ad Vincula dates
from the sixth century, when it was rebuilt by the Empress Eudoxiana. But long before that date there was
a church dedicated to St. Peter upon this site, and it
may even go back to apostolic days. The martyrology of St. Jerome gives under the date of 1 August:
" At Rome the dedication of the first church built by
the Apostle St. Peter". A priest of this church represented the Pope at the Council of Ephesus as one of
the legates, and signed the Acts: " Philipus ecclesiae
apostolorum presbyter ".

The tradition of the chains here preserved is also of
very high antiquity, at least as regards the Roman
chain, which was certainly at this church in the fifth
century. The Empress Eudoxiana brought a second
chain from Jerusalem, which also claimed to have
bound St. Peter. The story of the miraculous union
of the two chains is of later date.

Such, then, are the principal memories of the
Apostles which are preserved at Rome. Of St. Paul
there is practically no authentic trace except the place
of his martyrdom and his tomb. But the case is very
different with St. Peter. Here we have memorials of
various kinds connecting him with various parts of the
city. Recent excavations and research, so far from shak-
ing this evidence, have made it considerably stronger
than before, and it is probable that we have by no
means yet reached the limits of the light that archæology has to throw upon the subject. But even now

this at least seems clearly proved, that St. Peter must have lived a long time in the city, and have had relations with many residents in many quarters. Such results harmonize much better with the Church's tradition of a long pontificate largely spent at Rome, than with the notion lately put forward by Protestant scholars, that, although no doubt he came to Rome at the close of his life and there suffered martyrdom, there is no reason to believe that he had, at any previous time, ever visited the capital of the empire.

ST. PETER AS THE GOOD SHEPHERD

From examples in the Lateran Museum

From Marucchi's " I Monumenti del Museo Cristiano Pio-Lateranense " (Milan : Ulrico Hoepli)

CHAPTER II.

The Earliest Converts to Christianity.

IT was only natural that the first preaching of the new Gospel of Christianity should have appealed with especial force to the lower orders of society. The Apostles themselves were for the most part men of low estate, who lived by the product of the labours of their own hands. The Jews, to whom at the first the Gospel was preached almost exclusively, were everywhere, then as now, a people despised, outcast, and oppressed. As we examine the details of the Jewish colony at Rome in the first century we might almost be reading, under feigned names and changed conditions, an account of the Jewish community, as we know it in London or in any great European city of the present. There is, first, a small number of wealthy men, the leading financiers of the city, the forerunners of the Rothschilds and Hirsch of a late age, having little of Judaism about them except the names, and these, as they were among the richest, so also were among the most influential of Roman citizens. But these, as always, were but the few, and for the most part, then as now, the Jewish community was composed of the very poor. "They are a people born for slavery," says Cicero; "abominable among all the nations," says Seneca, who himself, however, was not always wholly unsympathetic. The Satirists, too, while they find in the Jewish practice of circumcision, in their institution of the Sabbath, and in their hatred for pork, an endless opportunity for witticisms, in general describe the Jews in terms of utter contempt; as beggars and rag-pickers; bartering tapers for broken glass; dirty and odorous; with swarms of ragged children; with no possessions but a basket, and no bed to lie on but a heap of straw.

If such were the conditions of the Jewish colonies of the dispersion, it is not to be wondered at that for the most part Jewish converts were not of a high rank. " Not many wise, not many noble," were chosen, as we know from St. Paul, and yet even among these some of the converts were of higher rank. A society which, like that of the earliest Church at Jerusalem, brought land and houses to be given to a common stock that the necessities of the poorer brethren might be relieved, obviously included many who were not of the poorest class, and what was true of Jerusalem was probably true also of the other cities in which the Jewish element was numerous.

The Slaves.

If we turn to the Gentiles we shall find that here again it was to the lower classes that the message first came. It was the fulfilment of our Lord's prophecy, the special characteristic of the Christian religion, that " the poor had the Gospel preached to them ". There was no class from whom the number of converts was larger than from the lowest social class of all—those who had no kind of political rights—the slaves of the Empire.

The slave in Roman law was a mere chattel of his owner. He was just a piece of property, which

must pay interest like any other, and from which profit
was extracted by systematic overwork. Some masters
were humane, others were not ; few had any interest in
their slaves except as means of profit, none troubled
about their moral condition or cared to help them in
any way. To such wretches as these the Christian
message of a common brotherhood and equality in the
sight of God made a strong appeal. They joined the
Church in crowds, and found themselves within her
borders almost in another world. Christian slaves
were allowed to partake of the Sacrament just like
Christian freemen ; they had an equal place in public
worship, and no longer lived in bestial concubinage, but
were duly married according to the laws of Catholicism.

Many of these Christian slaves, finding a new man-
hood and independence in the brotherhood of the
Church, carried on a keen apostolate in the homes of
their masters. It was a sore point with Celsus, as we
learn from Origen.[1] They stood firm under punishment and torture, and, to the astonishment of the
pagans, who could not understand such independence
in a slave, offered themselves rejoicingly for martyrdom.
The list of slave martyrs of the first two centuries is
indeed a long one. Felicitas at Carthage, Ariadne in
Phrygia, Blandina at Lyons, Sabina at Smyrna, Vitalis
at Bologna, Porphyrius at Cæsarea, Potamiana at Alexandria, Euelpistus at Rome ; these are but a few of
the many that might be quoted, but they are drawn
from every portion of the Empire. When slaves could
rise to martyrdom we need not wonder that they were
also found worthy to occupy the highest positions in
the Church. Hermas, the author of the " Shepherd,"
is said to have been a slave by birth, and if so, then
Pius, his brother, who sat on the throne of Peter about
the year 150, must have been one also. In any case it

---

[1] Origen, " Contra Celsum," iii. 44, 55.

is certain that this was so in the case of Callixtus a century later. He was born a banker's slave, and rose first to be Archdeacon of Rome, and then to be himself Pope on the death of his patron.

In no household among the nobles and leaders of Rome did the faith make more speedy progress than in the highest of all, "the household of Cæsar ".[1] We know that St. Paul himself had found

GRAFFITO OF THE CRUCIFIXION.
(From Marucchi's " Eléments d'Archéologie," Desclée De Brouwer et Cie.)

means to reach the slaves of the Imperial household, and the torch once lighted was never again extinguished. There were Christian slaves at Court under Commodus, and also under Septimius Severus, as we know from monumental evidence. Caracalla was brought up by a Christian nurse, *lacte Christiano educatus.*[2] The well-known *graffito* of the Palatine,

[1] " Bull. d' arch. crist.," 1863, p. 83 ; *cf.* " Inscript. Christianae," i. 9.
[2] Tertullian, " Ad Scapulam," 4.

now in the Kircher Museum, shows the ridicule and petty persecution to which these slaves were subjected. It represents a man with the head of an ass fastened upon a cross, and by his side another man in prayer, with the inscription, " Alexamenes worships his God ". It was found in the place where the pages of the Imperial household were educated.

At the commencement of the reign of Valerian Christians were so common in the Imperial household that Dionysius of Alexandria says that the place was like a church,[1] and a few years later, under Diocletian, the Christians belonging to the Emperor's own household who were executed reached very large numbers.

The Freedman.

Above the slaves we come to the lower class of freemen, those who had once been slaves themselves, or, at least, were among the poorer and less important of citizens. Here, again, great numbers had become Christians. Tacitus' account of the persecution under Nero shows us a great multitude, *multitudo ingens*, of sufferers, most of whom were apparently of this class, if we may judge from the kind of death to which they were condemned. The Acts of the Martyrs present us with many instances of this kind in later times : " The shepherds, Themistocles and Mamas ; the inn-keeper, Theodotus ; the gardener, Simeros ; the four stone-masons of Pannonia ; Philemon, the flute player ; Alexander, the charcoal-burner, who afterwards became a bishop ; while no doubt many others, whose profession is not given, might have answered as a martyr of Ephesus answered the judge who asked him what he was, ' A common fellow, living by my labours ' ".[2]

[1] Eus., " H.E.," viii. 6.
[2] Allard., " Dix leçons sur les Martyrs," Engl. trans., p. 156.

The monuments in this case fail in so far as direct evidence is concerned. Very rarely do the stones of the Catacombs preserve any memorial of the worldly rank of the dead. But indirect evidence abounds in the unscholarly character of the various epitaphs, misspelt, ungrammatical, and teeming with blunders. It is sometimes difficult to make out what is intended, so barbarous is the Latin of the texts. But assuredly it was no cultured people for whom such epitaphs were written, but rather for such as those whom Tertullian describes as the ordinary Christian of his time, " rude, uncultured, simple souls," [1] spending their lives at work and unable to attain to any learning or to aim at any refinement of living.

Here are a few examples :—

REGINA VIBAS
IN DOMINO
ZESV.

MARTYRES SANCTI
IN MENTE HAVITE
MARIA.

PETRUS ET PANCARA BOTVM PO
SVENT MARTYRE FELICITATI

A thousand more of like character could easily be added. But these are enough to bring home to us the fact that the great bulk of Christians, at any rate at first, must have been drawn from the less educated classes of society.

The Soldiers.

A class which deserves a word to itself, among those which yielded converts to Christianity, is to be found in the soldiers. In all ages there has been a

[1] Tertullian, " De test. animae," i.

somewhat unexpected connection between soldiers and
religion, and it is strongly marked in these centuries.
John the Baptist had baptized Roman soldiers in the
Jordan; our Blessed Lord had listened to the prayer
of the centurion of Capharnaum; the first Gentile convert was Cornelius, the centurion of Cæsarea. It was
among the prætorian cohorts at Rome that St. Paul
found his readiest listeners, and two at least of these
guardsmen, SS. Nereus and Achilleus, are numbered
among the martyrs of the Neronian persecution. In
the second and third centuries Christians were common
in the Roman ranks, so that Tertullian, who for the
most part exhibits a strong dislike and contempt for
the military life, appeals to the well-known fact as a
reason for allaying the rigours of persecution. "We
fight side by side with you," he urges, "we sail with
you, and till the soil together." [1] In Cappadocia, in
the time of Marcus Aurelius, even though we admit
some accretion of legend in the story of "The
Thundering Legion," it remains certain that this body,
the 12th Legion (*Fulminata*), was almost entirely
made up of Christians. [2] The massacre of the Theban
Legion [3] at the end of the third century, which is
narrated by St. Eucherius, involved several hundreds
of Christian soldiers. So, again, there were soldier
martyrs in the time of Diocletian in every province of
the Empire; in Italy, Mauretania, Spain, Asia, Egypt,
and on the banks of the Danube. This last persecution indeed actually began with an order that every
soldier in the army must either sacrifice to the gods or
else at once retire from the service, and soon went on
to harsher measures against them. Almost the last

[1] "Apol.," 42.
[2] See Harnack, "Die Quelle der Berichte über das Regerthunder
im Feldzuge Marc Aurel's gegen die Quaden," in Proceedings of
Acad. of Sciences, Berlin, 1894.
[3] Ruinart, "Acta Sincera," p. 290.

occasion on which Christian blood was shed, before the final peace of the Church was assured, was the instance of the forty Martyrs of Sebaste, exposed on the frozen lake in mid-winter by the orders of Licinius. The persecution of Julian the Apostate even later on gave us SS. John and Paul. Members of the military profession rank high among those who first listened to the Gospel message, and later gave their lives for the preaching of Christianity.

The Philosophers.

"Not many wise according to the flesh" are chosen, said St. Paul, and his words long remained true. Only in the second century do we hear of any prominent examples among the Christians of scholars and philosophers. There is no real foundation for the legend that St. Paul corresponded with and almost converted the great Seneca; though it is a singular fact that a tombstone has been found at Ostia which commemorates the death of a kinsman of his whose name proclaims him a Christian, MARCUS ANNAEUS PETRUS PAULUS. But similar conversions in the second century were numerous, especially in Egypt, and the Apologists are, most of them, men of this type who tried to use their talents at a time when such talents were highly valued at the Court of the Antonine Emperors, in order to bring about a lasting peace between the Empire and Christianity. The list of such is a long one at this period. Tertullian, Minucius Felix, and Cyprian were all of them lawyers who had practised in the courts; Aristides, Justin Martyr, Athenagoras, Pantaenus, and Clement of Alexandria are all names which stood high in philosophy. The medical profession gives us SS. Cosmas and Damian, Alexander of Phrygia, and many others. The whole is summed up in the words of Arnobius : " Orators and grammarians, lawyers, physicians, and philosophers, all have sought the Church, quitting contemptuously the doctrines in which they had formerly trusted ".[1]

The Nobles.

While the great body of the faithful must always have been drawn from the lower class there were always a certain number, and more than has generally been thought, who belonged to the higher circles of society. We can see this even in the early days of the Acts of the Apostles. The first convert made by St. Peter was an officer of the Roman army. At Cyprus the proconsul, Sergius Paulus, became a believer. At Thessalonica Paul converted " of noble women not a few ". At Corinth the treasurer of the city, Erastus, became a Christian. At Athens one at least of the famous Court of the Areopagites, St. Dionysius, was won to the faith. At Rome the recent discoveries of archæology put it beyond all question that the same was the case, only in a very much greater degree, and that among those who believed in the preaching of the Apostles were many of the very highest rank and nobility.

Tacitus[2] tells the story of one Pomponia Graecina, the wife of the general commanding in Britain, Aulus Plautius, who, about the year 47, gave herself over to perpetual mourning and refused to take any part in the pleasures that Roman society had to offer. In A.D. 58 she was brought before a kind of family court and charged with having joined an unlawful religion, but she was acquitted. Historians in all ages have been inclined to suggest that the " strange superstition "

[1] Arnobius, " Adv. gent.," ii. 55.
[2] " Annals," xiii. 12.

to which she was addicted was nothing else than Christianity, but there existed no proof of the fact till a few years ago, when a tombstone was discovered in a very ancient crypt in the cemetery of St. Callixtus bearing the name of Pomponius Graecinus. The Christianity of the grandson, or rather, perhaps, of the grand-nephew which is thus made certain, makes it exceedingly probable that it was from her that he derived his religion. We may put her down, therefore, as one of the earliest converts made in Rome by the preaching of St. Peter.

Pudens, who is mentioned by St. Paul in the First Epistle to Timothy, is another instance. By tradition he is said to have been of senatorial rank, and although not much more is known of him, we still have the church of Sta Pudenziana, the ancient *titulus Pudentis*, the titular church of Cardinal Wiseman and now of Cardinal Bourne, to witness to the fact of his Christianity. But if his history is obscure it is far otherwise with another of the same period, Manius Acilius Glabrio, Consul in A.D. 91 with Trajan, the proof of whose Christianity is another triumph of modern archæology. He was put to death by Domitian in A.D. 95, as a "contriver of novelty," which seems to mean the profession of the Christian religion. In 1888 his tomb was discovered in the Catacomb of Priscilla. Unfortunately the tomb had been wrecked by treasure-seekers in the seventeenth century, but enough remains to enable us to reconstruct its form.[1] It was a large crypt of rather unusual form, and the places for tombs within it were all arcosolia, or niches for sarcophagi ; there was not a single loculus of the usual cemeterial pattern upon the walls. Near to it was a large hall measuring nine yards by four and a half, which had formerly contained an altar, with spiral columns of giallo antico, now totally wrecked. Close by,

---

[1] " Bull. d' arch. crist.," 1889, p. 18; 1890, p. 97.

however, were discovered fragments of a marble sarcophagus, with the inscription :—

ACILIO GLABRIO . . . FILIO

still legible, in lettering of the time of Domitian or
thereabouts, so that no possible doubt remains that we
have here the family burying-place of the consul-martyr
and his family.   The date and the circumstances connected with the translation of his relics to Rome from
the place where he suffered are not known.   He was
not put to death in Rome itself, but in his place of
exile, which is not recorded.

The Acilii Glabriones were among the noblest of
Rome's noble families, but Christianity reached higher
still and did not stop till it reached the Imperial
family itself.   Indeed at one time it seemed almost
certain that before the first century had closed, a
Christian Emperor would be seated upon the throne
of the Cæsars.   The prefecture of Rome in the year
64 was held by one Titus Flavius Sabinus, the elder
brother of the future Emperor Vespasian.   In virtue
of his office he had no doubt to assist at, probably
even to arrange for, the terrible massacre of the Christians which Nero ordered in that year.   Such a task
must have been most distasteful to him, for he was, as
Tacitus [1] tells us, "a man of gentle nature, who ab-
horred bloodshed".   Possibly the scenes which he then
saw caused him to take an interest in men who could
suffer thus patiently, and may even have led him to
embrace the persecuted creed.   Anyhow, from that
time forward his nature seemed to have changed and
his contemporaries could not understand it.   He seemed
to them in his later years to have lost all his former
energy [2].   Prefect of Rome again under Vitellius in
A.D. 69, when his brother Vespasian was proclaimed

[1] Tacitus, " Hist.," iii. 60-75.
[2] In fine vitae segnem.

by the legions of the Eastern army, he failed to take advantage of the opportunity of securing the city for his brother by putting himself at the head of the guards and leading the rebellion against his master. Only as a last resort, when his life was in danger, did he take refuge in the Capitol. The Capitol was attacked by the mob, and, in the struggle which ensued, was burnt to the ground. Sabinus was seized "unarmed and not attempting flight," was dragged before Vitellius and forthwith murdered by the rabble, his mutilated and headless corpse being afterwards exposed on the Gemonian stairs. Truly a strange end, as Tacitus says, "for one who had fought for his country on five and thirty fields, and had covered himself with glory both as a soldier and in civil life".[1] Cowardice was felt to be out of the question with such a man, and most men contented themselves with the conclusion that it was due rather to his excessive anxiety not to shed the blood of his countrymen.[2] His innocence and justice, the historian adds, were beyond all question, nor can he find any fault to charge against him except a certain boastfulness of tongue.

Such a man we are naturally inclined to claim as a Christian, for this want of energy is precisely the charge which is constantly preferred against the Christians of the following century. It manifestly arose from the serious difficulty, if not the actual impossibility of reconciling civil duties with the claims of their religion. This difficulty confronted them as soon as they attempted to take any prominent part in political life, and made their position impossible.

We have, it is true, no absolute proof that Titus Flavius Sabinus was a Christian. Still here again, all reasonable doubt seems to be taken away when we

[1] Tacitus, "Hist.," iii. 75.
[2] Civium sanguinis parcum.

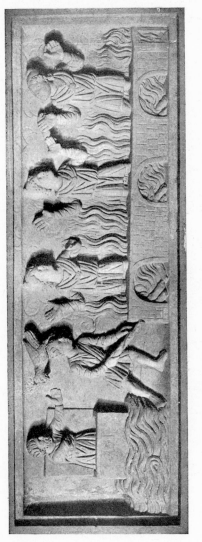

NOE IN THE ARK AND THE THREE CHILDREN IN THE FURNACE

From a sarcophagus in the Lateran Museum

From Marucchi's "I Monumenti del Museo Cristiano Pio-Lateranense" (Milan: Ulrico Hoepli)

find that, in the next generation, his son Titus Flavius
Clemens died a Christian martyr, and that his daughter Plautilla was also among the faithful. This
Clemens it was whose son and heir almost became the
first Christian Emperor. He had married his cousin
Flavia Domitilla, the granddaughter of Vespasian, a
niece of Domitian, and she like himself was a Christian. The sons of this pair were publicly desig-
nated by Domitian, after the death of his own infant
son, as the heirs whom he intended should succeed to
his throne. The hopes of the Christian community
in Rome must have run high, but, unfortunately, the
temper of the tyrant soon changed. Clemens was put
to death, accused, we learn from Dion Cassius, of
"atheism". Domitilla was exiled to Ponza, and the
two little boys not improbably shared their father's
fate, for they disappear from history, and we have no
clue as to what became of them. There remains,
however, to this day a splendid memorial and proof
that this elder branch of the Flavii really were converted to Christianity, in the family sepulchral chamber
at the entrance to the cemetery of Domitilla, containing some of the most ancient Christian tombs of
Rome, on one of which may still be read the Greek
epitaphs of one Flavius Sabinus and of his half-sister
Titiana.

Growth of the Church.

There is no need to carry the investigation further.
The facts we have given and the names we have
quoted are enough to prove that it was not from one
class only or from one single rank of society that
Christianity drew its earliest adherents. Every class,
every profession, every rank was represented among
them. Nor is it the least of the claims which the
Christian religion can put forward to prove its Divine

origin that it should so instantly and completely have occupied the entire ground, and shown itself so readily adaptable to the needs and yearnings of every race and every mind. Before even the first century had drawn to a close, the prophecy of our Lord had been abundantly fulfilled, and the little grain of mustard, smaller than all the seeds of the earth, had already grown up and become a great tree, the branches of which were overshadowing all the peoples of the world. Before the age of the persecutions was over, half the Roman world had become Christian. One would be amazed at the boldness of Valerian or Galerius in imagining that it was possible to crush such a body out of existence, were it not that we have in England and the North of Europe such vivid instances before us of what long-continued persecution was able to do in the way of stamping out Catholicism. By the end of the third century whole cities had become Christian. " People are astonished," wrote Porphyry at this time, " that towns where neither Esculapius nor any other god has now access should be stricken by a plague ! But ever since Jesus has been worshipped we have been deprived of all the benefits that the gods can give us." [1] At Edessa, Eusebius tells us, that " Christ only was adored," and he tells us also of another town in Phrygia, of which, unfortunately, the name has not come down to us, where, since all the inhabitants to a man were Christians, all were shut up in the great church which yet stood in spite of the edicts, and, the building being set on fire, the whole population perished in the flames, calling unceasingly on the name of the Saviour.

It was ever in the towns that the new religion spread first. The slow minds of villagers respond always but tardily to changes in religion, and the very name of

[1] In Theodoret, Migne, " P.G.," lxxxiii. 1152.

pagan remains to witness that this was the case. But by the end of the third century villagers also had become Christians in many places. In Bithynia, at the very beginning of the second century, Pliny tells how he was struck by the fact that villagers were among the number of Christian believers. Egypt was especially the home of rural Christianity. St. Dionysius of Alexandria, in a letter which Eusebius has preserved for us, tells us how, when once he had been taken prisoner, the news was carried to some feasters at a village wedding, whereupon all left their feasting, ran to the village where the bishop was held in captivity, fought the soldiers and put them to flight, and then effected the bishop's rescue. And when he was unwilling to make use of his freedom thus irregularly obtained, for fear of bringing evil upon his rescuers, they took him by his feet and hands, put him on a donkey, and carried him back to their own village.[1] The story brings back vividly enough some of the conditions of life during penal times in Upper Egypt, but it shows also how strong Christianity must have become if its adherents could dare to act in this way. Whatever they may have been in earlier days it is clear that by the end of the third century at least Christians had ceased to be the *latebrosa et lucifugax natio*, a people loving darkness and shunning the light, which pagans had formerly been accustomed to call them. The years of successful repression were over already, and a new courage had taken the place of former timidity.

[1] Eus., " H.E.," vi. 40.

CHAPTER III.

The Blood of the Martyrs.

IN the earliest years of Christianity the Roman power was not hostile to the new religion. In itself the Roman mind was one of large tolerance ; they had no desire to hinder any man from worshipping as he would, if only his worship seemed in their eyes to involve no danger to the religion of the State or to the continued political well-being of the Roman Empire. At the time when the Apostles arrived in the capital Rome was already full of every kind of Eastern superstition, and had welcomed all alike to its arms. Roman religion at that time cared little for dogma, nor was it anxious to investigate the credentials of any faith that offered itself for acceptance. It had come to be a strange medley made up of all kinds of elements ; Eastern as well as Western ; Asiatic and African no less than European. Already the better and keener minds of paganism were heartily tired of it, almost openly mocking at its claims to truth. Yet one and all were filled with the conviction that its maintenance was intimately bound up with the safety of the Empire ; and that, therefore, nothing that threatened it, or came into real competition with its claims, should be allowed even a chance of life.

The follower of Eastern superstitions in general seemed to the Roman in no way an enemy to the State religion. He was as ready to accept and to reverence the divinities of Rome as Rome was to reverence his own. For such there was no thought of persecution, for they constituted no kind of danger. On the contrary, these cults became popular among the Roman aristocracy, and the religions of Isis or of Mithra had open adherents highly placed in Roman society.

One religion alone stood out as obviously distinct and irreconcilable. It was the religion of the Hebrews, dispersed already over the whole world, although retaining their national life to some extent in Jerusalem. Monotheism is necessarily exclusive, and can make no acknowledgment of any divinity but its own. We should have expected, therefore, that Judaism would have been suppressed on this ground, that it ignored and despised the State religion of the Empire. Two considerations saved it from this fate. The first was its national character, for Rome was ever kindly disposed to the religions of the peoples she had conquered. The other was the severity of the demands that it made upon those who embraced it ; demands which were so bound up with its national character that they did away with all possible danger which might otherwise have arisen from tolerating it. Not many Romans after all were likely to become Jews, while to do so involved circumcision and the keeping of the Mosaic law.

For these reasons Judaism was invariably a *religio licita* under the Emperors. Rome felt she had nothing to fear from it. Far from persecuting the Jews or trying to stamp out their religion, Augustus had loaded the Temple with gifts, and after 71, when Judaism had ceased to possess a national centre at all, but existed only as a matter of religion and of race, emperor after emperor dispensed in favour of the synagogue the general laws which forbade Roman subjects to gather themselves together in meetings of any kind.

In the beginning, Christianity, to Roman eyes, seemed nothing more than a sect of Judaism, and, therefore, entitled to share in the toleration extended to the Jews. When the Jews themselves endeavoured to explain the situation, and to show that the new religion, although it drew its origin from their own, yet was entirely distinct from it in every way, the Roman magistrates would hear nothing of the plea. They told the Jews, as Gallio did at Corinth, that this was only a question of their own laws and ceremonies ; an internal dispute which they must settle amongst themselves, for Roman dignity forbade its officers to trouble about such matters. In the first years, therefore, not only was Christianity not persecuted by the Roman authority, but Christians were actually often protected by it against the Jews, who desired to invoke it on the other side.

This state of affairs, which we find pictured in the Acts of the Apostles, lasted on until the time of Nero. Gradually, no doubt, men had been becoming aware that the difference between Jews and Christians was not merely a surface difference, but one that was absolutely radical. The real change of opinion was gradual, but the actual and formal distinction between the two religions was made with startling suddenness, when in A.D. 64 Nero, possibly under Jewish influence, suddenly denounced the Christian inhabitants of Rome as having been the originators and fosterers of the great fire which had really been brought about at his own command.

The result of this distinction, which was now brought home to every individual in Rome, was that the Christians retained all the hatred and contempt which was felt almost universally for the Jews, and had added to it an opprobrium which was all their own. The common people had long been convinced that the Jews were really atheists and worshipped no God, because they knew that no image of any kind was allowed within the precincts of the synagogue. Much more were they now certain that this was true of the Christians, for these allowed no sacrifice of any kind, while the Jews, it was known, at least sacrificed at Jerusalem, even if they did so nowhere else. Strange stories, too, began to get about, concerning what happened at Christian meetings; stories which we can see well enough were based on misapprehension, or perhaps on deliberate misrepresentation, with regard to the kiss of peace, and to the sacrament of Holy Communion. Horrible crimes such as incest, promiscuous love, and cannibal feasts were freely imputed to them, and doubtless easily found believers. They were thought to possess the evil eye, to be constantly in league with the powers of darkness, and to be capable of casting a spell on any that might have offended them. Can we wonder that popular fury raged against them, and that it needed only a spark to set the passions of the mob alight? From the time of Nero onwards, not only the deliberate and calculated policy of the Emperor, but also the blind terror of the common people, demanded the extirpation of the Christians as enemies of the human race; men whom it was not safe to allow to live, for they were guilty of crimes which, if left unpunished, would call down the vengeance of the gods; crimes of which all alike were necessarily guilty by the very fact that they were Christians, *flagitia cohaerentia nomini*. That a Christian be not suffered to live, *Christianos non licet esse*, seems to have been the form, if not the actual words, of the law which initiated persecution; it was certainly the expression of the popular judgment. Everything which

went wrong was put down to their machinations, or
to the anger of the gods because their extermination
had been delayed. If the Tiber overflowed, or the
Nile was deficient, it was equally the fault of the
Christians; if the crops failed, or if pestilence raged, or
a Roman army was defeated, the populace had one
remedy and only one for every occasion, *Christianos
ad leones.* Throw the atheists to the lions.

This popular prejudice against the new religion is
the one great cause and explanation of the persecutions of the first century. Doubtless it was utilized
and fomented, again and again, by men in positions
of authority, who may, or may not, have shared in it,
but who were not above using it for personal ends.
That is the position with regard to Christianity which
is occupied by Nero and Domitian, the two great
persecuting Emperors before A.D. 100. Always, at
any time after A.D. 64, the unrepealed edict of Nero
—*Christiani non sint*—the only one of Nero's measures
which was excepted by the Senate when all the rest
of the legislation of that Emperor was repealed,[1]
was ready to be brought into force in response to any
popular clamour. But in the main, with some local
exceptions, the period from the death of Nero to the
reign of Domitian was a period of peace and of progress.

The Second Century.

With the beginning of the new century, however, we enter upon a changed state of affairs. In
112 Pliny the Younger was sent to take up the charge
of the Roman province of Bithynia, and found his new
district full of Christians. He was in some doubt as

---

[1] Et tamen permansit, erasis omnibus, hoc solum institutum Nero-
nianum (Tertullian, "Ad. Nat.," I. 7).

to the usual practice and procedure. His humane mind was appalled at the prospect before him if he began to enforce the letter of the law seriously against them. In consequence he wrote to Trajan, who had been Emperor for some fifteen years, to ask for guidance and direction. In reply Trajan sent the celebrated Rescript which was to govern the action of the Roman Government against the Christians for the next hundred years. Summed up very briefly it comes to this, that there was to be no inquisition, but those who were formally delated as Christians and confessed the charge were to suffer the full punishment ; if they denied it and were willing to offer sacrifice they were to be acquitted. The effect was to put Christians in an altogether peculiar position before the law. They were defended from vexatious persecution by the concession of what had apparently previously been denied, the ordinary right of freedom from molestation in the absence of a formal accusation. But their acquittal or condemnation was not to depend on evidence, but solely on their own words and actions when before the court. If they denied the charge and supported their denial by offering sacrifice of any kind to the gods, their acquittal was to follow as a matter of course, nor could they be further molested.

This decision, which, as we have said, dominated the law with regard to Christians for more than a century, shows plainly enough that Trajan had no more faith than Pliny in the charges commonly made against Christians in his time. Men guilty of hideous crimes, such as even pagans shuddered to recount, are not thus set free on the evidence of their own word, and without even a promise that they will for the future amend their ways. One only asks why it was that they were left liable to punishment at all, and why the edict against them, since in the eyes of their rulers it had

plainly ceased to be necessary, was not simply repealed.
The answer is to be found in the cold legal tempera-
ment of the Roman mind, which regarded such con-
stancy and perseverance in what was forbidden by law
to be itself an offence of great importance.   " I do not
doubt," wrote Pliny to Trajan, " that, whether they be
guilty or not, such pertinacity and inflexible obstinacy
deserves to be punished."   And Trajan replies in a
like tone, " If they are denounced and proved guilty,
they must be punished".   "You punish us," cries
Tertullian, " not because we are guilty, but because we
are discovered, although we ought never to have been
looked for."   " You forbid us to be searched for, it is
an acknowledgment that we are innocent, you condemn us when we are found just as if we were guilty."

Such was the state of the law throughout the second
century.   It was confirmed by Hadrian and other emperors in later years.   Under these conditions the
procedure of the courts was necessarily short and sum-
mary.   No evidence was ever called, for it was not
needed.   All that the magistrate had to do when the
accused was formally brought before him was to point
out the state of the law, that it did not allow anyone
to be a Christian, and then to put the question to the
prisoner whether or not he was an offender against
the law.   If he replied, "I am a Christian," it was
enough ; and sentence followed as a matter of course.   If
he denied the charge and would sacrifice to the gods,
there was equally no attempt to call evidence against
him ; but he was forthwith allowed to go free and unmolested.   The whole procedure was an exact reversal of the ordinary conditions of a trial.   Torture was
indeed applied, but it was not to extract a confession
of guilt, but to force the accused to deny his Christianity, and thereby to plead "not guilty " and obtain
his pardon.   One reads the account of the long series

of punishments inflicted by the magistrate, and one is apt to fail to realize his object. The whip and the dungeon, the rack and the scourge, were ordered not as additional punishments, but with the view of overcoming a culpable obstinacy and thereby saving the life which was otherwise forfeited to the law. The sentence on the martyr, when all other means had failed and at last it had to be pronounced, was always dependent on his own free will ; and the object of the law was always, in its own eyes, to save him from the result of his own reprehensible obstinacy.

The Third Century.

Such measures were not sufficient to crush out the new religion. On the contrary it grew and increased in influence. In 244 even the Emperor himself, Philip the Arabian, seems to have been a Christian, although he never openly avowed his religion. Persecution was almost at a standstill : formal delation of a Christian had become a rare event. Everywhere the numbers of Christians were increasing with the greatest rapidity. And then, at last, the Empire awoke under Decius to realize its own peril. The one thing that it dreaded, an *imperium in imperio*, an organized power that owed allegiance to a ruler other than itself, had grown up in the midst of it. The state paganism recognized at last explicitly, what her adherents had long subconsciously realized, that in Christianity she had found her connatural foe, and that either she must exterminate the professors of the new religion, or must herself be content to disappear before it until no place should remain to her anywhere within the borders of the Empire. The hour had come for the great struggle ; in Decius, and, later on, in Valerian, paganism had leaders wholehearted on her side, and set herself ruthlessly to the work of extermination. Persecution enters upon the third and most terrible of its phases.

Decius does not appear to have been by nature a cruel man, but he was a strong conservative and re-actionary, quite convinced that the safety of the Empire was bound up with the maintenance of the state religion. His first effort was not to exterminate the Christians, but to intimidate them and force them to renounce their religion. Hence his new edict, issued in the year 250, ordered that everywhere, throughout the Empire, on a single fixed day, all Christians were to come, and, when their name was called, to offer sacrifice in some form or other. A certificate was to be given to all who complied, and all who afterwards could not show that certificate were to be brought up for punishment, and if necessary for death. The persecution was not bloodthirsty; the object was by no means extermination; every effort was made to induce Christians to comply with the new law, the endeavour, as St. Jerome puts it, was "to destroy souls but not bodies".[1] But even so, the sum of suffering must have been terrible. The magistrates had every power of applying torture to enforce compliance, and did not hesitate to use it. Thousands of Christians were detained under conditions worse than death, in prisons "darker than darkness itself . . . where night reigned eternal, and never visited by the light of day".[2] They longed to die, but death would not come to them, and they were left in these conditions often for months and even years. Who will deny them the title of martyrs, even when their sufferings did not end in death? "You live in a dark abode," wrote Tertullian to such confessors, "but you are a light to yourselves;

---

[1] "Vita Pauli erem.," 3.
[2] Prudentius, "Peristephanon," v. 245.

you are bound with chains, but you are free for God; you inhale a fetid air, but yourselves are an odour of sweetness; you await the sentence of an earthly judge, but you yourselves shall be the appointed judges of the nations."[1]

The Decian persecution was but short-lived, and soon died away—only to be succeeded five years later, in 257, by the yet more terrible persecution of Valerian. The policy of this Emperor was the same as that of his predecessor; the revival and protection of the old paganism as the uniting bond that held the political fabric of the Empire together, and prevented it from breaking up into separate fragments. Christianity as a disintegrating force hostile to this must be destroyed. He saw, however, the uselessness of acting as Decius had done, and of attempting to destroy a world-wide religion at a single blow. His aim, therefore, was to proceed by slow degrees, but to destroy the enemy unrelentingly and without exception.

His first attack was on the bishops and clergy of the Church. For these death was decreed in every case of refusal to sacrifice. Next the churches, and even the burial-places, which till then had remained unmolested under the sanction of the laws, were to be confiscated and destroyed. *Christianis non sint areae.* Lastly, those among the nobles and richer men who were Christians were to be degraded to the ranks of the people, their property confiscated, and any political privileges they may have possessed were to be disregarded. In this way by striking at the heads Valerian thought to destroy the whole body. Of the common people he recked nothing. Deprived of their leaders and of the clergy on whom their religion depended they would be unable, he calculated, to maintain an inde-

---

[1] Tertullian, " Ad martyres," 2.

pendent existence. In any case, it would be time enough to attack them when the earlier measures had been successfully carried through to their conclusion.

Such was the design of Valerian, and in several ways it differed from all previous attacks on the Church. For the first time money enters into the question ; goods are forfeited, families are impoverished, and the public treasury is enriched at their expense. For the first time the public property of the Church is confiscated, and the Christians are denied the privileges guaranteed to all by the common law. For the first time the poor and simple are left untouched—it was on them that the worst horrors of previous persecutions had fallen—and the rich and prominent had to bear the brunt of the battle. The attack was fierce while it lasted, and the loss to the Church, both in souls and in property, must have been very great, but it did not last long. In 260 Valerian was taken captive by the Persians, his son Gallienus reigned in his stead, cancelled the edict of his father, and once more restored to the Church the cemeteries and meeting-places of which she had been deprived. " And the land had rest forty years."

The Fourth Century.

At the beginning of the fourth century things had been so long undisturbed, and Christianity enjoyed such wide and universal freedom that men had almost forgotten that such a thing as persecution had existed, and could at any moment, under laws yet existing, be called into fresh existence. Churches were built both in the East and in the West ; Christians no longer troubled to hide their religion, but professed it openly ; the chance of renewed persecution seemed so far off as to be practically negligible. And then, from a blue sky,

came suddenly the greatest and most violent storm
that Christianity had ever yet been called to meet—
the persecution of Diocletian, the fiercest and the last
of the persecutions of the Church. It was the dying
struggle of the old pagan religion, fighting in sheer
desperation for a continuance of its former predominance. There is little of the old dignified procedure of
outraged law vindicating its majesty. It is rather a
savage war of extermination that spared neither age
nor sex nor character. The idea had got possession
of the dominant party that the only way to destroy
Christianity was to kill the Christians. The very
weakness of which they were conscious was the cause
of the savagery of their proceedings, for they felt that
to spare the Christians was to set the seal to their own
political effacement. It is the invariable position which
leads up to a Reign of Terror, and in this instance we
have no exception to the general procedure.

Each year from 303 to 306 edict after edict poured
forth from authority against the Christians, who by
this time must have numbered nearly half of the
population of the Empire, while in many places, especially in Asia, they commanded an actual majority.
The persecution assumed the character of a veritable
civil war. Churches were destroyed; copies of the
Sacred Scriptures and liturgical books were searched
for and burnt; every person of whatever degree
throughout the whole Empire was ordered to sacrifice;
priests and bishops were everywhere to be put to
death; cemeteries were confiscated; and the property
of recusant Christians everywhere held forfeit to the
State. In some places every scrap of food offered
publicly for sale was sprinkled with water from the
sacrifices, and at the doors of the baths and other
public edifices sentinels were stationed with commands
to insist that all who entered should offer incense to

the statues of the gods. The net was cast so widely that none it would seem could possibly escape it, and Christian blood, in greater quantities by far than at any previous epoch, was shed freely for the cause of their religion. So deeply did the iron burn into the consciousness of the faithful in Egypt that to this day the Copts and Abyssinians count their years, not, as all other Christians from the birth of Christ, but from the accession of Diocletian, the *Era of the Martyrs*. At Mastar there has been found an inscription which commemorates the terrible *dies thurificationis*,[1] the days of violence when all Christians were forced to offer sacrifice or to die as the result of their refusal.

The persecution bears the name of Diocletian, though it was not from him that it really proceeded. Galerius, his colleague and successor on the throne, would bear the title of persecutor with far better right, and Maximin, the third of the tetrarchy, was perhaps the keenest persecutor of all. Diocletian had abdicated in 305 and Galerius died in 311, but still the persecution dragged on until the years of horror had been fulfilled. Then at last came the battle of the Ponte Milvio; the victory of Constantine as the avowed champion of oppressed Christianity; the edict of Milan, and the peace of the Church. The long series of persecutions had come at last to an end, and after 300 years Christianity had won for herself a legal right to existence. For centuries had "the kings of the earth stood up, and her rulers taken counsel together, against the Lord and against His Christ,"[2] but all to no purpose. So far from exterminating Christianity, persecution had only served to make it known. Christians in 312 were more numerous than ever. The blood of the martyrs had proved indeed to be,

---

[1] De Rossi, "Bull. d' arch. crist.," 1875, pp. 162-75.
[2] Ps. ii. 2.

according to the oft-quoted saying, the seed of the Church.[1]

The Relics of the Martyrs.

The Church was not unmindful of the great debt which she owed to those who had, during the years of persecution, so faithfully given their lives rather than be untrue to her teaching. The name of Martyr, at first applied to any who bore witness for the faith, became, as years went on, the highest of her titles of honour. It was jealously kept for those whose blood had actually been shed, or who at the least had undergone rigorous imprisonment and torture; and it gave, *ipso facto*, the right to the religious veneration of Christians everywhere. Even before their death those who were about to witness for the faith were held in such dignity that they might ask what they would and none could deny them, least of all the Lord for whom they were about to suffer. Such was the first origin of the whole system of " indulgences," which was to grow to so much larger proportions in the Church. " The martyrs gave grace to those who were not martyrs, and received the lapsed back into communion " (cf. Eus., " H.E.," v. i. 40 ; ii. 7, 8). As soon as a martyr was thrown into prison, others crowded around him to beg his intercession on their behalf. St. Cyprian even felt himself bound to protest against the honours that were paid to them. " What martyr," he asks, " is greater than God, or more merciful than the Divine compassion, that he should fancy that we are going to be preserved by no greater aid than he can afford us." [2]

By Roman law the bodies of those who were

[1] Tertull. " Apol.," 50.
[2] Cyprian, " De laps,," c, 20,

executed were ordinarily given up to the friends of the culprit. Joseph of Arimathæa in this way obtained for burial the body of Christ, and in like manner, in the earlier persecutions, Christians obtained leave to gather up for burial the remains of the martyrs. The account of the funeral rites accorded to St. Cyprian will show us with what solemnity it was possible, even when persecution was raging, to carry out their burial. They buried him, we read, *cum cereis et scolacibus, cum voto et triumpho magno.* Torches and candles were carried by his side, hymns and psalms were sung in his honour as the long procession made its way to the appointed tomb. There, in the depth of the earth, in the dark passages or chapels of the catacombs, year by year and month by month, as the recurring anniversaries came round in long rotation, the Holy Sacrifice was offered in the presence of the faithful, above the body of the martyr, as the most appropriate of all possible altars. When the peace of the Church made it possible to offer Mass in the light of day and without concealment, the conscience of the Church had become so accustomed to the martyrs' tombs as the only places of sacrifice, that to this day she orders their relics to be placed in every altar, and the service of the consecration of an altar is, practically speaking, nothing else than the burial with all the accustomed ceremony of a Christian martyr who has died for his religion.

After the year 258, the year of the persecution of Valerian, the old clemency which waged no war on the dead was formally withdrawn from the Christians. Henceforward the bodies of the martyrs were exposed to the dogs and the vultures, and every effort was made to prevent the faithful from obtaining them for burial. In the persecution of Diocletian the Christian slaves of the palace were buried as soon as their torments were over, but very soon the Emperors ordered that they should be dug up and cast into the sea " because if they remained in their sepulchres very soon they would be worshipped as deities.[1] Datianus, the governor of Valentia, in like manner ordered the body of St. Vincent to be thrown into the sea " lest the Christians should honour his relics as those of a martyr ".[2]

Such barbarous treatment of their heroes roused the Christians everywhere to superhuman efforts to save the relics. " In the reign of Decius the faithful of Pergamos 'stole in order to put them in safe custody' the charred bones of Carpos, Papylos, and Agathonice.[3] In Valerian's persecution the Christians of Tarragona broke into the amphitheatre in the darkness and recovered the still smoking remains of Fructuosus and his deacons.[4] Under Diocletian . . . the Christians disguised themselves as sailors and set out to fish with their nets for the bodies of Philip and Hermes, who had been cast into the Ebrus."[5] At a much earlier time we find the same zeal constantly exhibited, as for instance, at the martyrdom of St. Polycarp. "We took up his bones," we read in the letter of the Smyrnaeans, "bones which are more precious than precious stones and finer than refined gold, and laid them in a suitable place, where the Lord will enable us to gather ourselves together, as we are able to celebrate in gladness and in joy the birthday of his martyrdom." If nothing more remained the blood was collected, and handkerchiefs and other objects soaked in this were solemnly interred. The following

[1] Eus., " H.E.," viii. 6.
[2] " Passio S. Vincent," 10.
[3] " Mart. Carpi," at end.
[4] " Acta SS. Fructuosi," 6.
[5] Allard, " Dix Leçons sur les Martyrs ".

inscription, found in Numidia, commemorates an event of this kind :—

```
                                    . . . DEPOSI
TIO  CRVORIS  SANCTORVM  MARTYRVM.
QVI  SVNT  PASSI  SVB  PRESIDE  FLORO  IN  CIVI
TATE  MILEVITANA  IN  DIEBVS  TVRIFI
CATIONIS . . .¹
```

In the catacombs the tombs of the martyrs can sometimes be recognized by little vases of blood, *vas sanguine tinctum.* These, however, even when accompanied by the palm branch, cannot be regarded as an infallible token of martyrdom. The only sign which is really certain is the word *Martyr*, or, at the least the letter M cut in the stone after the martyr's name. So well was this recognized in ancient times that persecutors sometimes broke into the cemeteries and effaced the letters from the graves in order to prevent religious ceremonies from taking place. But numbers still remain to us even to-day. In the cemetery of Priscilla, the most ancient of all, the letter M is all that we find. The first epitaph that bears a date is in the cemetery of St. Hermes, the tomb of St. Hyacinthus :—

DP. III. IDVS SEPTEBR YACINTHVS MARTYR.

In 1849 and 1852 De Rossi recovered the two pieces of the primitive epitaph of St. Cornelius :—

CORNELIVS MARTYR
EP.

At Lyons, to give one of many similar examples outside of Rome, there is a stone which records the burial of a woman of high rank (*clarissima*) :—

A TERRA AD MARTYRES.

¹ "Bull. d' arch. crist.," 1876, plate iii.

The Title of Martyr.

The title of martyr with all that it conveyed to the minds of the faithful was not given lightly. We are far enough, of course, in those early times from the modern rules concerning canonization of the saints. Usually the title to religious veneration was based simply on popular acclamation. But in the case of the martyrs care was exercised by the Church authorities from a very early time. Lists were kept in every church of those who had died for Christ and whose memory was worthy of honour. No heretic or schismatic, or one who had sought his own death, might be inscribed upon these lists even if his death for Christ was undisputed. The right of placing a name thereon was reserved to the Bishop; and till this had been done the title of martyr could not be given. This process was called *vindicatio* and was very strictly demanded. So at Carthage during the time of the persecution of Diocletian, a certain matron called Lucilla was called in question for having paid religious honour to one who " though a martyr had not yet been vindicated," *cujusdam mortui, etsi Martyris, sed necdum vindicati.*[1] Nor could any stronger proof be brought of the rigour with which the discipline was enforced than is afforded by the tombstone of Pope St. Fabian, which is still *in situ* in the catacomb of St. Callixtus. There the title, as any one can see, was not inscribed at the time, although space was left for it. There was no doubt of his martyrdom, the clergy of Rome made it the subject of an encyclical letter, but there was no bishop to sign the *vindicatio*, for the see was vacant and remained vacant for eighteen months. When at last Cornelius had succeeded, and the *vindicatio* could be carried through, the relics had long been

[1] Optatus, " De schism. Dom.," i. 16.

buried and the stone was already *in situ*. Hence, when the title of martyr was added the two letters MR were cut less deeply into the slab, lest the stone should be split by the force which was then applied. Nothing could speak more eloquently either as to the greatness of the honour that was thus held to be done to him, or the care of the Church that such honour should not be given to any that were not worthy to receive it (see Plate).

How true it has proved to be that " God has chosen the foolish things of the world to confound the wise, and the weak things of the world to confound the things that are mighty ".[1] The great ones who condemned them have long since passed into oblivion and no man recks of their sepulchres, but the martyrs are honoured and venerated with an honour that grows with the ages. " We fools accounted their lives madness and their end to be without honour. But now their lot is among the saints and they are numbered among the children of the Highest." [2]

[1] 1 Cor. i. 27.   [2] Wisd. v. 4.

VIRGIN AND CHILD.   FROM THE CATACOMB OF ST. PRISCILLA

From Marucchi's " Eléments d'Archéologie" (Desclée, De Brouwer et Cie)

EPITAPH OF ST. FABIAN

From Marucchi's " Christian Epigraphy" (Cambridge University Press)

CHAPTER IV.

The Collegia and the Catacombs.

IN nothing was the law of ancient Rome more remarkable than in its care for the memorials and burying-places of the dead. Such places acquired, by the very fact that men had been there laid to rest, a quasi-religious and sacred character. Henceforward no man might offer them for sale, if by so doing he would alienate them from the families of those who were buried there. Even if a whole estate changed hands, the *loca religiosa* did not pass with it, and it was never lawful to deny to any family the right of access to the tombs of its ancestors. This jealous care was not confined to the burial-places of the rich ; the tombs of the poor, and even of slaves, could claim the same right ; nor was the protection of the law refused to the last resting-place of those who had suffered as transgressors against it. Only in rare instances was there added to the sentence of death the further penalty of the denial of funeral rites. In all other cases all men, once they were dead, were equal before the law, and it was the duty of the Pontifices to watch over their tombs and to see that no man disturbed in any way the arrangements which had been made.

These arrangements for keeping alive the memory of the dead were often very elaborate. Ordinarily they included memorial feasts, to be provided out of money left for the purpose, and to be eaten at the grave of the testator. Not seldom it was further enacted that sacrifice should be offered, and that those who had benefited by the will should be present at the sacrifice on certain specified days in every month, or at least in every year. For these purposes an upper chamber was often provided above the vault in which the dead were laid, an *edificium superpositum* as it was often called, which served as the meeting-place on these mournful occasions. Sometimes land or gardens were set aside by a testator for the purpose of providing the entertainment and of keeping his tomb in order and repair. Here is an actual instance: "These gardens shall always serve my ashes. I shall appoint guardians to feast on my birthday on the income they provide and to throw roses on my tomb. I will that they shall never be alienated nor divided." [1]

The Collegia.

Such were the arrangements of the rich in order to keep their memory from perishing. Poorer men could naturally do much less than this, but many could and did make some provision. Some bought themselves land for a grave while they were yet living, or at the least a niche in some one of the public *columbaria*, where the urn containing their ashes could be deposited. But the usual way in which the poorer Romans provided for their last obsequies was by means of mutual co-operation. They formed themselves into burial guilds and societies by whom they could be cared for after death had taken place. It is said that the Roman soldiers used to make regular contributions out of their pay for this purpose ; and it is certain that

[1] " Corpus Insc. Lat.," v. p. 843. The inscription is at Grazzano.

members of the various trades and professions had each
their own burial clubs.[1]

Nothing was more carefully regulated in the later
days of the Republic and throughout the times of the
Empire than the right of joining together in any form
of guild or society. Such organizations, it was feared,
might be used for seditious purposes and militate
against the good order and government of the State.
From the days of Augustus onward it was forbidden
to form any new association of a private character
without the special leave of the Senate, which was
very rarely given. Under Trajan such liberty was
even more narrowly restricted. Pliny has left on
record his absolute failure to get permission to enrol
a body of firemen, even though he proposed to confine
their numbers to 150 and promised to be very careful
in making his selection.[2]

To this general and strictly enforced prohibition
one exception and one only was allowed. It was the
provision to be made by the poor (*tenuiores*) for their
funeral rites. Such men were allowed to meet together
and to make monthly contributions to be applied for
this purpose.[3]

The classical instance which has come down to us
of such burial clubs among the pagans is to be found
in the celebrated inscription discovered at Lanuvium,
now called Città Lavinia, in 1816. It recites the law of
the Senate by virtue of which it was allowed to exist,
and also the special conditions insisted on; that it
should not meet oftener than once a month, and should
be formed *bona fide* for the provision of burial facil-
ities. Then follow the statutes of the club. Every

[1] Brownlow, " Roma Sotterranea," i. p. 66.

[2] Pliny, " Ep.," x. 97.

[3] Marcianus, " Institut.," iii. ; " Digest," xlvii. 22, 1. Cf. Momm-
sen, " De Collegiis et Sodalitiis Romanis," and De Rossi, " Roma
Sotterranea," iii. 509.

member as an entrance fee had to give a keg of good wine and pay a sum of about sixteen shillings. After that his monthly subscription was to be about four-pence. If at his death his subscriptions were long in arrear he was to forfeit all rights, but if his subscriptions were paid up and he had paid for a long time the club provided a sum of about thirty shillings out of which the expenses of his funeral were met. Suppers were to be given on fixed days—including the birthdays of the founder of the club, and of some of his relations, and the anniversary of the foundation of the club itself. Bread and wine and small fishes (*sardae*) were to be provided for this purpose. Then follow certain fines and other regulations for the due management of the club. The date of the monument is about A.D. 133.

This may serve as a typical instance of the burial *collegia* which were existing everywhere in the second century. Any family or body of persons who had some common bond of unity might form themselves into such a *collegium* and draw up statutes for the due administration of any property which the *collegium* might hold. As members of such a college they gave themselves a new name by which they might be known. Thus the members of the *collegium* which met at the sepulchre of Annius Phylles were known as the Phylletians, while in another instance they were known as the Syncratians. These are pagan instances, but it is quite likely that there were Christian parallels, and it may well be that this is the true explanation of a stone which still remains in a beautiful vault in the cemetery of St. Callixtus, which bears the single word inscribed upon it EVTYCHIORVM.

Christian Burial Guilds.

Indeed it is not hard for us to see how admirably this law was adapted to the special needs of the

Christians who wanted to find a loophole which would allow them to meet together for religious worship without thereby rendering themselves liable to be punished for unlawful assembly. As we go on to consider the history of the Christian catacombs we shall constantly find ourselves faced by details which seem to show that it was precisely in virtue of this exception to the general law that these singular burying-places came into existence.

We must, however, be on our guard against assigning to this system of burying guilds an influence in the development of Christianity greater than that which it actually possessed. Mgr. Batiffol[1] has made an attack on this ground on the whole position on this point which was taken up by De Rossi. "How could Christianity," he asks, "being a religion, have concealed itself under the name of small funeral *collegia*? Who could have been deceived by the device? How could it have been possible for Christian worship, with its meetings held every Sunday and often during the week, to be protected by a legislation which allowed the *collegia* to meet only once a month? How could Christians who were admitted to communion in any church they visited, have complied with a legislation which forbade anyone to belong to more than one such college?"

Arguments of this kind would be decisive if anyone were contending that the use of such *collegia* was the only way in which Christian worship was carried on, or that the Christian Church as such applied for recognition in this way. It is no argument at all against the more moderate position put forward by De Rossi and maintained by his followers, which is simply that some Christians at special times of persecution seem to have availed themselves of the loophole provided by

[1] " Primitive Catholicism," pp. 35, 36.

the law. We may admit readily enough that Christianity itself was neither a *collegium* nor a collection of *collegia*, but it still remains possible and probable that Christian *collegia* did exist and quite probably existed in considerable numbers. Of at least one instance we have positive proof in an inscription recording a "*Collegium quod est in domo Sergiae Paulinae*".[1]

The Catacombs.

From the first, Christians set their faces resolutely against the pagan practice, which had become almost general, of burning the dead. "Christians execrate the funeral pyre and condemn burial by fire," says Minucius Felix. It became necessary for them, in consequence, to make provision for the large numbers for whom burial was needed, and this was done, as we shall see, in a very remarkable way.

It was not infrequent among the richer and nobler Roman families for the older custom of burial to be retained, and a great many monuments have come down to us which show us the way in which this was commonly done. The most important are subterranean vaults surmounted by an upper chamber above ground, and many remain in a more or less dilapidated condition along the Via Appia and the Via Latina. But in other cases subterranean chambers and passages were cut out in the solid *tufa* rock with horizontal shelves or arched recesses in the walls upon which the dead bodies might be laid.

Both these plans were adopted by the Christians in their turn. The tombs of St. Peter and St. Paul, in the Vatican and on the Ostian Way respectively, were examples of the first kind, funeral vaults containing only a single sarcophagus, and in the case of St. Peter's

---

[1] "Roma Sotterranea," i. 209.

surmounted by an upper chamber or chapel. The second plan, however, was that which was almost universally followed, especially when the commencement of persecution made a burial above ground increasingly difficult. It was given so great an extension by the Christians that it has come to be looked upon as exclusively their own, whereas in point of fact both pagan and Jewish catacombs are, even now, known to exist.

At the first these catacombs were private burying-places, on the property of individual Christians. A few wealthy and charitable persons did precisely what some of their pagan neighbours were doing, and set aside a plot of land for their own resting-place and for the burial of such as they might choose to allow to be brought there. Hence the oldest cemeteries bore the names of private persons ; of Lucina, or of Priscilla, or Domitilla, to name three of the most famous, all of which bear the names of women of rank ; or, again, of Prætextatus, or the Cœmeterium Ostrianum, so called from the family of the Ostriani to whom the property belonged.

All the cemeteries present the same characteristics, and set the type for the great development which followed in later centuries. The extent of those now existing is enormous, and if all the galleries within three miles of Rome could be stretched out in a single line it has been computed that they would equal the whole length of Italy itself. They are cut out in the rock in various levels, one under another, with staircases leading from one to the next ; are about 3, or at most 4 feet in width and 8 or 10 in height. All the way, on both sides, the walls are pierced with horizontal niches like berths in a ship's cabin, one above another, and every niche was made to contain one or more dead bodies. Here and there the galleries widen, or access is given by a door to a larger excavation, forming a chapel or place of worship, generally containing the tomb of at least one of the martyrs. Now and then a tomb may be seen of a more pretentious character. An arch has been cut out and recessed in the rock and an oblong space excavated beneath it to receive one or perhaps more bodies, and the wall under the arch is often decorated with paintings. These more costly tombs are known as *arcosolia*, and it was upon them, when they contained the body of a martyr, that the Holy Mysteries were celebrated. The other graves are closed in with simple marble slabs set vertically, and bearing the name of the person buried within, with, in many cases, some Christian emblem or words of aspiration.

In the oldest instances the inscription is often Greek.

At first, as has been said, these cemeteries were provided by private persons and remained in private hands. But as years went on this could no longer be the case. It became necessary for the authorities of the Church to take the administration of the cemeteries into their own hands, in order to make proper provision for the burial of the faithful, who had now reached great numbers. By the time of Zephyrinus this had been done, for we learn from the "Philosophumena" of Hippolytus (ix. 7) that this Pope, in A.D. 203 or thereabouts, "entrusted his deacon Callixtus with the government of the clergy and set him over the cemetery". One at least of the great cemeteries of Rome was, therefore, already the property of the Church as a corporate body, and this seems to have been recognized by the State, which could hardly have been ignorant of the fact. The description given us by Tertullian of the way in which the management was carried out shows us that, in fact, advantage had been taken of the law concerning *collegia* which has already been described, and which was the only way in which the Church at this epoch could have ventured to hold corporate property at all. "Each person," he says, "contributes a small sum once a month, or whenever he likes, and if he likes and has the means to do it. . . . All these contributions are, as it were, pious deposits ; for they are spent, not on feasting, but on feeding the hungry, or *burying the poor*, or orphans, old men and shipwrecked persons ; and if any are condemned to the mines, or exiled, or in prison, provided only that it be on account of God's sect, these also become the foster-children of their confession."[1] The Acts of St. Lawrence provide us with a well-known instance of the way in which this constant relief of distress was carried out among Christians at this period.

The cemetery which we know now as that of St. Callixtus, from the name of its first administrator, became the official cemetery of the Church and the most important of all. Other cemeteries also became, later on, Church property, but this always kept the predominance, and in it accordingly were laid to rest the remains of the Popes who died during the next hundred years, from A.D. 217 to A.D. 314, from St. Zephyrinus to St. Melchiades, with only two or three exceptions due to the active persecution which was raging at the time of their deaths. The first part of this period was a time of peace, and the Church under the protection of the law concerning *collegia* was able to carry on her worship and to bury her dead without let or hindrance of any description.

The Catacombs Confiscated.

Then in 258 came the withdrawal of this privilege. The Emperor Valerian knew the use that was being

[1] Tertullian, "Apol.," c. 39.

made of the catacombs to carry on Christian worship
unmolested, and to prevent it he excluded Christians
from the benefit of the universal law. We see the
result of his action at once in the communications
made by the Prefects in Egypt and elsewhere to the
Christian bishops. "Neither to you nor to any other,"
wrote the Prefect of Alexandria to Dionysius the
Bishop, " is it permitted to hold assembly or to enter
the places which you call your cemeteries." It
was unlawful to hold assemblies, and, therefore, the
Holy Mass could no longer be celebrated under these
conditions.

The catacombs of Rome still bear the traces of these
terrible years of the persecutions of Valerian and of
Diocletian during which worship was thus proscribed.
Thus we can often trace the precautions which were
taken to protect the martyrs and their relics from profanation. The bodies of St. Peter and St. Paul, as we
have seen, were taken from their tombs at night and
hidden away in the place known as the Platonia at
San Sebastiano. Similar precautions were taken in
the catacombs themselves. Some of the galleries
were filled up with earth and rendered impassable.
Sometimes the lower steps of a staircase were cut off
so as to be full of peril to any who were not in the
secret. Sometimes, again, walls were built to separate
catacombs that had been joined, and fresh entries were
made, hidden in unlikely places and leading to the
shrines only by long and deceptive ways. Every pre-
caution was taken to render surprise difficult and thus
to enable the faithful to meet as before for purposes of
worship.

These elaborate precautions were, however, often
unavailing. Either by the treachery of false brethren,
or in some other way, the Roman soldiers not unfre-
quently succeeded in breaking in at the very time that

Mass was being celebrated. Pope St. Xystus was thus discovered saying Mass at the cemetery of Præ-textatus, was hurried off to the seat of judgment, and then was brought back to the place of the Mass and there - beheaded. On another occasion on the Via Salaria, when a great multitude of the faithful had been seen to enter the catacomb to venerate the tombs of St. Chrysanthus and St. Daria, the entrance was hurriedly built up by the Roman soldiers and great masses of earth were heaped in front of it, so that all who were within perished miserably by starva-tion. Long afterwards St. Damasus, touched by the piteous tale, sought for and discovered the spot, and found there not only the relics of the martyrs—skele-tons of men, women, and children lying on the floor— but even the silver cruets they had taken with them for the offering of the Mass. He would not have them touched, but left all as a memorial of Christian for-titude, and they could still be seen through a window in the sixth century. It is not even impossible that the spot may yet again be discovered in our own times.

But except in the few bad years of active persecu-tion these things did not happen. After the death of Valerian, Gallienus gave back the cemeteries and things went on much as before. Indeed the ecclesi-astical administration became, in the first years of the next century, still more minutely organized. Mar-cellus (308-9) is the name especially connected with these reforms. In spite of the shortness of his reign and ·the great difficulty of the times in which his lot was cast, in the midst of the Diocletian persecution, he divided up the *tituli* or parish churches into seven regions, and connected them with the cemeteries, so that each parish had its own burying-place. Henceforward the priests of the *titulus* in the city had the manage-ment of the cemetery that went with it. We see the fact proclaimed in many an inscription of the fourth and later centuries. The following, from the cemetery of St. Domitilla, may stand as an example :—

> ALEXIUS ET CAPRIOLA FECERVNT SE VIVI
> IVSSV ARCHELAI ET DVLCITI PRESBB.

Alexius and Capriola made this in their own lifetime, with the permission of Archelaus and Dulcitus the priests.

The Fossors.

The excavation and keeping in repair of all these miles of galleries demanded an immense deal of labour, and this was given over to a particular class of men, the *fossores* or diggers, who carried out their charge with great difficulty and self-denial because of the want of air and the pestilential atmosphere in which they laboured. Hence they were always regarded as worthy of especial honour, as sacrificing themselves for the common good. The work was one which required a good deal of skill and knowledge, as otherwise the galleries would continually have been breaking into one another, and great confusion would have resulted. It was no mere hard and unpleasant labour that they performed, but a highly skilled and technical art, which had its own special danger in the risk of martyrdom inseparable from it. Hence they ranked immediately after the clergy, and were well-known and trusted officials of the Church, charged with the important duty of caring for the tombs of the martyrs and those of others who were buried within the area of their charge.

There is a very famous tomb in the cemetery of St. Domitilla which bears on it the representation of one of these *fossors*, Diogenes by name. He bears the pickaxe on his shoulder, the special sign of his office, by which the *fossors* may always be recognized in any representation of the period, and is surrounded by the implements of his craft, hatchet and hammer, chisel and compasses, mallet and lamp. It bears the inscription : " Diogenes the Fossor, buried in peace ".

At a later date, after the peace of the Church and towards the end of the fourth century we find the *fossors* apparently almost in the position of owners of the catacombs, selling the graves and registering the title to them. But in earlier times there is no trace of this, and rich and poor seem for the most part to have been laid in similar graves, and without payment of any kind. It is another evidence for the existence of the *collegia*, of which we have spoken.

But this last carries us on to later years than our present subject allows. For the present it must suffice to have sketched out in outline the circumstances which brought the catacombs into existence, and enabled them to be carried on for the use of the Church and the preservation of her worship. To the religious services of the catacombs how much do we owe of that which we are enjoying to-day. The whole Christian calendar as regards the anniversaries of saints had its rise in the meetings at the tomb of the Martyr on the *natalitia* or anniversary of his martyrdom ; the relics of the saints built into every Catholic altar carry us back to the times when their tombs were the only places where Mass could lawfully be celebrated ; the consecration of a new altar to this day takes the aspect of the burial of a martyr. The lights in our churches, especially at the reading of the Gospel at High Mass and in the course of processions, have, in the opinion of many, no other origin than the darkness of the subterranean chapels in which Mass was then

5

said. Everywhere, as soon as we begin to make serious inquiry into origins, we find the glorious ceremonial of the Church of to-day has sprung from those humble beginnings which alone were possible for Christian worship when it had to be carried on under the conditions of persecution, in subterranean vaults and chapels excavated far down in the very bowels of the earth.

CHAPTER V.

The Christianizing of Rome.

THE fierce battle between the old paganism and the new Christianity for the possession of the Empire, which we know by the name of the persecution of Diocletian, could not be continued for a very protracted period. The final issue was really decided before that persecution ever began, for Christianity was already, by the end of the third century, too widely diffused and accepted by too many adherents to be successfully stamped out. A *modus vivendi* had to be reached in one way or another if the Empire itself were not to perish, weakened as it must have been by this long internal strife; and many of the less fanatical thinkers on the pagan side must have been asking themselves anxiously, about the year 312, in what way such a *modus vivendi* could best be discovered.

It came, as we all know, by the conversion of Constantine the Emperor to Christianity. Not that Constantine thus suddenly and openly avowed his change of faith. That would have been too dangerous a thing to do; nor, perhaps were the Emperor's opinions at that time sufficiently clear and settled to justify him in such a procedure. At first the whole affair bore the aspect of mere political expediency, and only by degrees was it made manifest to how great an extent the Emperor's own religious beliefs were involved.

The whole matter at a later date became obscured by stories, such as that of the famous vision of the cross before the battle of the Milvian bridge ; stories which no doubt have a real historical foundation, but which have nevertheless been exaggerated, and tend sometimes to take possession of the imagination and thus to obscure the true historical sequence of events. Here archæology comes in, and is able by indisputable monumental evidence to fill in some at least of the *lacunae* left by the documents of history.   It shows us not so much Christianity triumphing over paganism, as Christianity and paganism living side by side, both enjoying the protection and favour of the State.

The persecution had been brought to an end, and peace had been finally given to the Church by the famous Edict of Milan in 313.   The effect of this edict was simply to annul the existing laws against Christianity and to put the Christian religion into the category of *religiones licitae*, religions which were recognized and permitted by the State.   It put an end to the condition of affairs which had continued ever since the time of Nero, according to which Christianity was not only not permitted to exist, but was absolutely forbidden under the strongest penalties ; but it did nothing further.   The issuing of the edict did not mean that the Emperor had himself embraced Christianity, or even that he intended to do so.   It only meant that the Christian religion now attained the position which the Jewish, for example, had always been allowed ; that it was a permitted religion, whose votaries were free to worship as they pleased, and to build churches and own property, not merely by means of legal subterfuges as they had done in the past, but of absolute right and without any fear of molestation.

This consideration enables us to understand how it was that the Edict of Milan was the joint act of

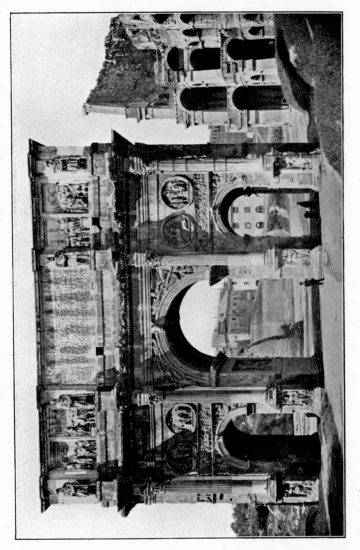

ARCH OF CONSTANTINE AT ROME

Constantine and Licinius. Whatever Constantine
may have thought in his heart of Christianity in 313,
Licinius was a convinced pagan. He, at least, had no
leanings towards the religion to which he was thus
giving a legal status. It was a mere political act, the
extension to the Christians, for the common good of
the Empire, of privileges and rights which could no
longer safely be denied to them, and it could, therefore, be the act of pagans just as easily and con-
sistently as of Christians or converts.

The edict is divided into two parts. The first lays
down the principle which was to govern future action;
the second is devoted to a detailed instruction on the
methods according to which the properties which had
been confiscated from the Christians during the years
of persecution were to be given back. Henceforward,
every man, without distinction of rank or of nation-
ality, is to have free choice and liberty in religious
matters; and he is not only not to be persecuted or
compelled in matters of conscience, but to be left
without any kind of molestation or annoyance. Of
course, the freedom of the Christians is what is aimed
at and intended, but the edict is not openly drawn up
from a Christian standpoint, for if it had been, Licinius
could not have signed it. So there is not even any
explicit mention of the name of God, and the powers
of heaven are spoken of in obscure terms—*Quicquid
est divinitatis in sede coelesti*, Whatever divinity reigns
in heaven. By these means the object was fully
attained; the perfect liberty of the Christians was
completely ensured wherever the edict had force and
was not frustrated by the action of Maximin the third
Emperor; but, at the same time, the personal religious
opinions of Constantine and of Licinius were in no
way compromised.

As a matter of fact, however, Constantine was

already prepared not only to allow the Christians freedom, but also to give them the benefit of his own patronage, though he was not willing to go so far as to undergo baptism and take upon himself the responsibilities of being an actual professing Christian. He wrote letters to the Bishops of Africa which implied that he held the Christian faith. "I, too, expect to be judged by Christ," he wrote in 313. In this same year, too, he handed over the palace of the Lateran to serve as a residence for the Christian bishop and as a meeting-place for Christian worship; and it was there in the next year, 313, that a council was held against the Donatists and sentence was finally issued. But still the Emperor, however well inclined privately, was not openly Christian. The coins of this period, and indeed of his whole reign, are still entirely pagan, which is no doubt largely accounted for by the fact that coinage was a privilege of the Senate, and the Senate was still overwhelmingly pagan. Constantine was still Pontifex Maximus and practically supreme head of the State religion. He could not give up this dignity without lowering himself in the eyes of a large number of his subjects, nor could he allow it to be held by any other. While paganism retained any strong life at all it was impossible that an Emperor should not be Pontifex Maximus and keep its regulation in his own hands. That had been seen long ago by Tertullian, when he said that no man could be at once Cæsar and Christian.[1] But what had seemed so impossible to the clear-sighted and logical African, was feasible for a politician of less uncompromising character, and the double rôle of Christian Emperor and Pagan Pontifex was successfully sus-

---

[1] "Apol." xxi. "Sed et Cæsares credidissent super Christo, si aut Cæsares non essent saeculo necessarii, aut si Christiani potuissent esse Cæsares."

tained throughout a period of fifty years both by
Constantine himself and by his sons. It was probably
precisely this political necessity which made Constantine put off his baptism to the very last moments of
his life.

The Position of Constantine.

Even in 313, when he triumphed over Maxentius,
Constantine had refrained from any actual part in
pagan sacrifices. He gave the people their games and
rejoicings, but there is no mention of any visit on his
part to the Capitol. In 315, when the Arch of Triumph
was erected in his honour near the Colosseum, the
question of the inscription to be placed thereon brought
up the same difficulty once again. An examination
of it will show how the question was solved by means
of a compromise. He would not admit of the older
phrases such as *diis faventibus*, by the favour of the
gods, but, on the other hand, the Senate and the
Roman people would have rebelled against any as-
cription which would openly exclude the ancient
deities. The actual phrase adopted, *instinctu divinitatis*, is capable of interpretation in either way, though
it is certainly more easily explained as referring to the
one true God. But it passed the Senate, as far as we
know, unopposed, and takes its place as the first
explicit statement in an official monument of the
momentous change which had taken place.

Now and again the history of the times allows us to
catch a glimpse of the very difficult position in which
Constantine found himself through the endeavour to
belong to both camps at once, and to be at heart and
by profession a Christian without definitely breaking
first with paganism. The old religion was far stronger
in the West than in the East, and he was able to do
more for Christianity and against paganism at Con-

stantinople than he could at Rome; a fact which in
itself may have influenced him in setting up his new
capital.   Constantinople was definitely founded as a
Christian city, in contradistinction to Rome which remained chiefly pagan; almost all the population which
crowded into her became Christian—at least nominally
—and yet even there we find strange outcrops of pagan
ritual.   When the city was dedicated in 330 the ceremony was only half Christian.   The chariot of the Sun-
God was set in the market-place, and above it was
placed the cross of Christ.   So also the statue of the
Emperor was allowed to remain in heathen temples
until quite a late period in his reign.   Some historians
have concluded from these and similar facts that
Constantine was never wholly Christian at heart, but
really favoured some kind of syncretic religion.   The
political difficulties of the position, however, are quite
sufficient to account for all.

We must remember that until 323 Constantine was
not reigning alone, but in union with his colleague
Licinius, who was tending more and more to be inclined to favour a pagan reaction.   The position of
Constantine was, therefore, peculiarly difficult for these
first ten years of his reign, and it was quite impossible
for him to declare himself in any way an open enemy
of paganism.

The Building of St. Peter's.

All that he could do in these years was to raise up
Christianity and to help it not only to repair the
damage of the last years of active persecution, but also
to show itself in a more dignified way to be at least
the rival and the equal of the State religion.   For this
purpose, beyond anything else, a great central cathedral and place of worship was urgently required.
Christianity could not rival the pagan religion in the

Restoration of the Old Basilica of St. Peter's at Rome

From the drawing by the late H. W. Brewer

number of her churches—that was obviously impossible—but she might at least have just a few which could bear comparison with even the finest of the pagan temples.   Until this was done she could never make an adequate appeal to the minds and imagination of the people, but must always be content to occupy a merely subordinate position.

This idea, coupled no doubt with a genuine desire to do honour to the Prince of the Apostles, was probably responsible for the determination, arrived at as early as 315, to build a vast basilica over the tomb of St. Peter on the Vatican.   It was built in a great hurry, and in as economical a fashion as possible.   The Emperor was not yet throwing the whole of his influence on the side of Christianity.   The foundations of the Circus of Nero were cleverly utilized for the new church, and this must have saved many thousands of pounds.   The materials, too, were almost entirely second-hand, and had done duty before in pagan edifices.   The notebooks of Antonio da Sangallo the younger, an architect of the time of the destruction of old St. Peter's in the sixteenth century, which are preserved in the Uffizi at Florence, give details about a large number of the columns, and show us what a nondescript collection they must have been ; drawn from every quarry and decorated in every style of art. Grimaldi says that he could not find two capitals or two bases alike.   Many of them bore pagan inscriptions, which showed the uses they had previously been put to.   In one place a bust of the Emperor Hadrian was visible between two acanthus leaves.

The old pagan edifices were still in active use, and the collection from such sources of material for a large building had not become so easy as was afterwards the case, and this must have hampered the builders very considerably.   Still the building of St.

Peter's marks an epoch, in a way which is less true of
the earlier handing over of the Lateran palace, and
the dedication of its basilica as the cathedral of Rome.
Christians now had a vast edifice of their own ; one
which could in some sort vie with the great pagan
temples ; and they were in consequence able to carry
out public ceremonies with fitting pomp, and to take
their proper place as members of a great and world-
wide religion.

But even after the building of St. Peter's, and
for many a long year to come, Christianity, so far as
externals are concerned, could only take a very subordinate place when she was compared with the
glories of paganism.   It is hard for us to form an
adequate idea of the magnificence of Imperial Rome,
even in its decline under Constantine.   The regionary
catalogue compiled by him, about 334, enumerates no
less than 423 temples still existing.   When Constantius,
Constantine's second son, came to Rome from Byzan-
tium for the first time in 357, he was utterly over-
whelmed by the greatness of the city.   At that time
the old buildings were still intact, and the work of
destruction had not yet been commenced.

Constantine's Later Years.

A period of greater freedom for the Emperor began
in the year 323, when the battle of Chrysopolis put an
end to the reign of his pagan coadjutor Licinius, and
left him alone in undisputed power.   Accordingly we
find that a fresh note was struck in his proclamation
to his new subjects in the East.   Licinius at the end of
his days had attempted a pagan reaction, and his
doings during this period had now to be reversed.
The situation was in many points very like that which
obtained at the time of the issuing of the Edict of

Milan in 313, eleven years before, but the phraseology is curiously and instructively different. One feels that the author of the two documents is free, in 323, in a way in which he was not in 313. The policy, however, remains just the same. There was no attempt to reverse the position, and to persecute the pagan. Constantine made very little difference, all through his reign, between pagans and Christians. The inscriptions at Rome show us a great number of nobles invested during his reign with such high positions as consulates or prefectures, while still remaining prominent members of the pagan religion; pontiffs, augurs, and so forth. Hence it is necessary to receive with much hesitation the statements of Christian historians of a generation or two later, which represent the Emperor as having declared war against the temples and forbidden the sacrifices. By that time Constantine had been elevated to the rank of a Christian hero, and he was accordingly represented as having acted as these writers thought a Christian Emperor ought to do, without much reference to the question whether he had actually done so or not. With the monuments and inscriptions we are on ground that is safer than that which is afforded by these statements of the historians.

It is true that in 329 we have a proclamation directed against soothsayers and tellers of fortunes. But this and all similar acts of legislation were rather aimed at acknowledged abuses than interference with real religious worship. With regard to this last, even where pagans were concerned, Constantine maintained complete tolerance not only up to the death of Licinius, but also throughout the fourteen remaining years of his reign. But at the same time he was not careful to hide his own personal preference for Christianity nor his growing dislike of paganism. Nor was he at all inclined to any general tolerance on the lines on which most moderns would conceive the idea. He had no notion of any complete liberty of conscience which would allow every individual to do exactly as he pleased in religious matters. More and more the question presented itself to him as one between the old State paganism on the one hand, and the Catholic Church on the other. He had set himself to bring about a *modus vivendi* between these two great powers, so that the Empire might not be devastated by civil war, and he had entirely succeeded. A policy which had done so much was not one to be changed, even though the difficulties inseparable from it might stand in the way of the Emperor's own realization of all that he desired in the matter of religion. But it did not necessarily mean any kind of toleration for those outside the Church, who yet claimed to be in some sort Christian. For heretics and schismatics of any kind Constantine had no mercy. Valentinians, Marcionites, Novatians, and Donatists had, none of them, anything to hope for at his hands, except the confiscation of their goods and the destruction of their chapels. Their action could only act in the direction of weakening the Church in the great struggle for supremacy upon which she had formally entered—the final issue of which, in spite of the personal patronage of the Emperor, was as yet very far indeed from being determined.

We may refer to the last years of his life the very definite statements of the inscriptions at St. Peter's and in other churches of Rome. At St. Peter's we know of two, both of them very explicit. One was in the actual crypt wherein the body of the Apostle reposed, and probably is there to this day, though the crypt has been closed and no eye has rested on it for more than a thousand years.

CONSTANTINVS AVGVSTVS ET HELENA AVGVSTA
HANC DOMVM REGALEM SIMILI FVLGORE CORVS-
CANS
AVLA CIRCVMDAT.[1]

This is as it stands in the text of the "Liber
Pontificalis," but it does not make sense. De Rossi,
in order to give it an intelligible meaning, suggested
the insertion of the words *auro decorant quam* between
regalem and *simili.*

The other inscription was on the triumphal arch
over the altar, where Constantine was himself depicted
in mosaic at the side, offering the basilica, to our
Lord.

QVOD DVCE TE MVNDVS SVRREXIT AD ASTRA TRI-
VMPHANS
HANC CONSTANTINVS VICTOR TIBI CONDIDIT AVLAM [2]

Whatever he may have done in the crypt where
no unfriendly eye could see it, it would have been
most unwise for Constantine to put such an inscription as this openly in any Christian building, at any
rate until after the death of Licinius. It seems almost
more probable that it was not really put there till after
Constantine's own death.

After Constantine's Death.

The picture, then, which we have to make for ourselves of the Rome of the fourth century is one of two
great religions existing side by side in a more or less
peaceful fashion. The older religion is still the
religion of most of the aristocracy, and of a little more
than half the people; and is still in undisputed possession of all the old treasures, temples, and monuments
of its earlier greatness. The other and newer religion

---

[1] Barnes, "St. Peter in Rome," p. 185.
[2] "Inscr. Christ." ii. 345; see also Barnes, op. cit. p. 164.

is the religion of the Emperor himself, and of the other half of the population, but not of very many of the upper classes. It has a few fine buildings and a great many churches scattered about the city; but in the main, and as compared to its rival, it is still a poor religion and almost without endowments. But it is constantly growing, and growing at the expense of paganism by conversions from its ranks; growing even when paganism once more lifted up its head and attempted fresh persecution under Julian the Apostate; growing rapidly and continuously both in power and in influence and in numbers; while the opposite is true, and true ever increasingly, of the older pagan worship, most of whose members by the end of the fourth century clung to the old religion much more through innate conservatism, than from any real conviction of its truth or love of its doctrines.

In 408 came the first great attack of the barbarians from the North, the Goths under Alaric, followed by the Vandals under Genseric in 455. Then came a long fifty years of every kind of disaster—scarcity and famine, pillage and siege, pestilence and massacre. The old religion had not vitality to stand against such a series of catastrophes. The fifth century is the period of its fall and of its final disappearance, a fall of which we know hardly any details.

In 408 when the Goths appeared before Rome, we find paganism still apparently vigorous and flourishing. Externally at least, it was as strong as ever it had been. Sacrifice was offered solemnly at the Capitol, and the Prefect of Rome and the whole Senate was officially present.[1] When this availed nothing the treasures of the temples, still intact and unplundered, were drawn upon in order to pay to the Goths the ransom of the city. It was the first great blow of

[1] Sozomen, ix. 6; Zosimus v.

the kind that paganism had received, and from it it never recovered.

The Goths were Christians after a sort, that is they were Arian sectaries. The Christian churches, therefore, were respected to some extent by them, especially the basilicas of the great Apostles. The precincts of St. Peter's, and also those of St. Paul's, were made into sanctuaries of refuge, and were untouched by marauders. In any case Christian churches at this time cannot have offered a booty in any way comparable to that which was ready for sacking in the pagan temples, and this alone will have secured them comparative immunity.

When the barbarians returned to their native North, they left behind them a paganism already writhing in the agonies of death. Christianity at last had the field to itself, and henceforth appears as the only religion of Rome ; but it was a Rome far different from that of the past. The old splendid edifices remained, although in a state of ruin, and these one after another were taken possession of for purposes of Christian worship. Slowly and by degrees, after the lowest depths of misfortune had been touched at the end of the sixth century, the new Rome began to arise out of the general chaos. Had it not been for the Papal See and the consequent necessity of preserving a centre for the work of the government of the Church, Rome might have disappeared almost as completely as Babylon or Nineveh. But this was not to be. As it was she was spared that final degradation. Henceforth, accordingly, she is to be known as the Eternal City, for she now has a title to greatness which cannot be taken away from her, as the capital of Christendom. Under Gregory the Great a new Rome begins to come into being out of the ruins of the old. It is no longer imperial, the seat of Empire has not been there since

330, and will never come back to it again. Rome
papal has come into existence, ruled over by the successor of St. Peter, occupying the buildings and filling
the place of the older Rome; it is a Rome no longer
in any sense pagan—the old heathen deities have
scarcely a single real adherent within the walls of the
city—but a Rome in which all are in union, where
government and people alike profess but a single religion and aim at a single ideal, the religion and ideals
no longer of the paganism that is ended, but those of
which she is henceforward always to be the centre,
the worship of Christianity and the ethical ideals of the
Catholic Church of Christ.

PART II.

CHAPTER I.

The Symbolism of the Early Church.

IT would not be possible to get any clear idea of the true meaning of such relics of the past as the paintings of the first three centuries on the walls of the catacombs at Rome without a preliminary study of the symbols which were at that time agreed on. At a time when persecution was still constant, and when the Church was surrounded on all sides by hostile pagans, it was clearly quite impossible to depict the mysteries of the Catholic faith in any obvious manner. That was forbidden if in no other and more formal fashion, at least by the thought of the reverence due to the Sacraments of the Church, and by the memory of our Lord's injunction that men should not cast the pearls of their faith to be trampled under foot by swine. Consequently, a whole language of Christian symbolism came into being, in which all Christians were duly instructed—a language which to them spoke eloquently enough, and which was readily available for the instruction and edification of the youngest neophyte, while to the pagan intruder it told nothing and seemed to be nothing more than ordinary and somewhat uninteresting decorations,

The Old Testament.

The stories of the Old Testament furnished a large field from which this symbolic language could be drawn. In themselves they were harmless and free from danger, so far as persecution was concerned, since Judaism was one of the permitted religions. But their significance was not limited to the historical facts they commemorated. They spoke also to the Christian of the inner meaning of which those stories were typical. Thus the figures of Adam and Eve standing on each side of the tree in whose branches the serpent is entwined, spoke to them, indeed, of the Fall of man, but also of the second Adam and of man's Redemption. So also the picture of Noe and the Ark recalled the Deluge, but spoke far more eloquently of the Church outside of which was no salvation; of baptism by which men were to be saved from the flood of destruction and brought into the Ark of safety; and of the Resurrection through which men should be brought to a new heaven and a new earth from which all danger should be taken away and all persecution be absent. So, again, the representation of Abraham and Isaac spoke of the sacrifice of the Cross, and of the Lamb slain from the foundation of the world; Moses striking the rock told of Peter and the new Covenant, in which the waters of baptism gush from the side of the rock, which Rock is Christ. At Podgoritza (the ancient Doclea in Dalmatia) a singular glass vase of the fourth century was discovered some years ago. It is now in the museum of M. Basilewski at Paris. On this vase the usual scenes of the Catacombs are drawn, but their Christian meaning is made clear, in a way which was not possible during the years of persecution, by explanatory legends attached to each scene. The scene of Moses striking the rock is thus commented

JONAS AND THE WHALE

From a sarcophagus in the Lateran Museum

From Marucchi's "I Monumenti del Museo Cristiano Pio-Lateranense" (Milan : Ulrico Hoepli)

on : *Petros virga perquodset, fontes ciperunt quorere*—[1]
Peter struck with his rod, the fountains [of grace]
began to flow.

This striking of the rock is not the only scene in
which we find Moses depicted in the catacombs.
Sometimes, perhaps more frequently, he is represented with the roll of the law, as the means through
whom the Law of God was made known to the Jewish
people. Here again he is a type of Peter, the lawgiver of the New Covenant, and, accordingly, he frequently bears the well-known features of the Apostle.

The story of Jonas is another which is constantly
represented. Here the application is, of course, clear
enough, "the sign of the prophet Jonas". He is represented in three separate ways : as being swallowed
by the whale—as cast up by the whale on the shore
—and as sitting under the gourd. The symbolism of
the first two scenes is clear enough, and was explained
by our Lord Himself (Matt. XII. 40). For as Jonas
was three days and three nights in the belly of the
whale, so also had the Son of Man to be a like time
in the tomb before He could pass to the glories of the
Resurrection. The symbolism of the third is less
obvious. It is interesting to note that the tree represented is always the melon or gourd, never the ivy
(*hedera*) of the Vulgate. Rufinus criticized St. Jerome
for this novelty and appealed to these very paintings
of the catacombs to prove his point (St. Jerome, " Epist."
cxii.). The symbolism is apparently of death, or at
least of the uncertainty of human life and the vanity of
human ambitions.

The Three Children in the Fire was another very
favourite subject. The story is one which was admirably calculated to comfort and inspire those who re-

---

[1] Petrus virga percussit, fontes ceperunt currere. For a sketch
of the vase in question see p. 104.

called it in those days of constant persecution, when any might be called upon at any moment to witness with his life for the faith which he professed. The same may be said of another subject, which is scarcely less frequent, the Prophet Daniel cast into the den of lions. It is hardly necessary to look for any further symbolism, but the attitude of the prophet, who is usually represented as an "*Orante*," in the position of prayer with outstretched arms, seems to point to a desire to identify him with the Redeemer, struggling with the powers of darkness on the Cross of Calvary.

Mythology.

Another field of symbolism was offered by the legends of heathen mythology. We should have expected that the early Christians would have shrunk from exploiting this field when the legends still had life and power for evil among their heathen neighbours. But it was not so, and we find in the catacombs at least one representation of pagan mythology, placed there, it may be, partly with the design of misleading heathen visitors as to the nature of the building in which they found themselves, but mainly with the idea of edifying the faithful by the inculcation of the truths of Christianity which it could be used to illustrate. This representation is that of Orpheus with his lyre, charming the animals by the music which he plays. We meet with it in the Catacombs of Domitilla, of Priscilla, and of St. Callixtus, so that it is among the most ancient of these symbolic devices, but it is far from common. The Christian signification is obvious enough. Just as Orpheus by the power of music had tamed the wild beasts and brought them to his feet, so also has Christ, the true Orpheus, tamed and subdued mankind, fallen to the

level of the beasts, by the sweetness of His doctrine
and the attraction of His example.

Animals and Birds.

A still more important field of symbolism is offered
by certain objects of common life, especially animals
and birds. The representation of these could tell
nothing to anyone who was not of the brotherhood,
while to the initiated Christian they could be made to
speak with the utmost eloquence and depth of meaning. A real understanding of the witness of the
monuments, and the support which they give to
Catholic doctrines, depends so much upon a full com-
prehension of the ideas which these symbols conveyed
to a Christian of the early centuries, that we must go
into some of the more important symbols with a
certain carefulness of detail.

The Lamb.

The lamb is used as a symbol sometimes of our
Blessed Lord, sometimes of the faithful Christian. It
is most common in the frescoes, which are among the
most frequent of all, representing the Good Shepherd
carrying a lamb on His shoulders while two others
run at His side. There is an ancient prayer recorded
by Muratori (" Lit. Rom. Vet." i. 751) which explains
the meaning of this picture very beautifully : " We
pray God . . . to grant him a merciful judgment,
having redeemed him by His death, freed him from
sin, and reconciled him to the Father. May He be
to him the Good Shepherd and carry him on His
shoulders. May He receive him among the followers
of the King, and grant him a share of perpetual joy
in the fellowship of the saints." The lamb on the
shoulders of the Good Shepherd is the Christian at

the moment of death, or the sinner just reconciled to the Church, the two others at His feet are those who have never strayed or who have already come to the safety of heaven.

Sometimes the lambs are being watered by the Apostles, or themselves, again, represent the Apostles, who surround the true Lamb standing on a little mount in the midst of them. In the crypts of St. Lucina is a stone which is one of the most ancient of all, and dates from the first century. It bears the lamb lying under an anchor, and is, as it were, a veiled representation of the crucifix. At Nola a similar carving had the explanatory inscription, SUB CRUCE SANGUINEA NIVEO STAT CHRISTUS IN ALBO, bidding all who saw it to see Christ represented in the lamb and the cross in the anchor above it.[1]

One more variation of this symbol deserves special notice. It consists in the depicting with the Lamb, or sometimes with the Good Shepherd, a vessel containing milk. The meaning is, of course, that as the Shepherd feeds his lambs with milk, so also does Christ feed the souls of the faithful in the Holy Eucharist. Or, in case the application is specially to the souls of the dead, the milk must be taken to symbolize the joys of heaven and the Beatific Vision.

The Ram.

The ram must not be confounded with the lamb in Christian symbolism, but has a distinct meaning of its own, founded upon that passage of Genesis in which, after Abraham had given the proof of his faith and obedience in his willingness to sacrifice his only son Isaac, if such should be the will of God, a ram caught by its horns in a thicket provided the fitting substitute.

---

[1] St. Paulinus of Nola, "Epist." 32, 17, Ad Sever; Migne, 61, 339.

The ram, therefore, denotes our Lord as the Redeemer, and St. Prosper draws out the symbolism in connexion with the Crown of Thorns and other details of the Passion.

The Stag.

Here, again, the meaning is fixed by a passage of the Old Testament. The allusion is to the Psalms : *As the hart panteth after the fountains of waters, so my soul panteth after Thee, O God* (Ps. xli. 1). It represents, therefore, primarily, the Gentile or Jewish converts, thirsting after the waters of baptism, though sometimes also the stag is represented with the chalice, and, in that case, the longing is for the refreshment of the Christian soul by the Sacrament of the Holy Eucharist. From the natural timidity of the deer was drawn the lesson that Christians must fear and shun moral dangers, or, sometimes, in protest against the error of the Cataphrygians, that Christians had no right to seek martyrdom directly, but when persecuted in one city must fly to another. Tertullian uses it in this sense. " I have known some of their pastors to be lions in time of peace, and deer in times of persecution."

The Dove.

The dove, as a Christian symbol, draws its significance from the story of the Baptism of Christ, and hence its primary meaning is the influence and work of the Holy Spirit. Thus St. Gregory, in times rather later than those we are discussing in this book, is generally shown with a dove on his shoulder, to denote Divine guidance and inspiration. The symbol occurs frequently in connection with baptism, in which case its meaning is obvious. As a symbol of martyrdom it expressed the need of Divine grace to enable

the soul to endure suffering. As a secondary meaning, it symbolizes the Church, the organ through which
the Holy Spirit works on earth. When two doves
appear the symbolism may represent, according to
Macarius (" Hagioglypte," p. 220), the Church of the
Circumcision and that of the Gentiles.

On a sarcophagus, or on other funeral monuments,
the dove signifies the soul of a Christian indwelt by
the Holy Spirit. Hence it tells of the peace of the
departed soul, especially when, as is generally the case,
it bears an olive branch in its beak. The reference
here is, of course, to Noe and his departure from the
ark, and hence it denotes faith in the resurrection.
Occasionally funeral lamps were made in the form of
a dove for this reason. Two doves on a funeral monument often denote the conjugal love and affection of
those who were buried there.

The dove in flight is the symbol of the Ascension of
Christ, and of the entry into glory of the Christian soul.
Similarly, the caged dove denotes the soul detained in
the body and held captive during the period of mortal
life. Speaking generally, the dove as a Christian emblem signifies always the Holy Spirit, either personally
or in His works. Hence if it denotes a Christian soul
it contemplates that soul as indwelt by the Holy
Spirit; and especially, therefore, as freed from the
toils of the flesh and entered into the glory of everlast-
ing happiness.

The Fish.

The fish is by far the most important and the most
frequent of all Christian symbols. Its special attraction for the faithful is derived no doubt from the famous
acrostic formed from the initial letters of the Greek
word Ἰχθυς. This single word, thus interpreted, summed up the whole of Christian theology concerning

our Lord. It told of His name and office, of His Divine and human nature, of His priesthood, and of His work as Redeemer. Ἰησοῦς Χριστός, Θεοῦ Υιός Σωτήρ—Jesus Christ, the Son of God, the Saviour. Every baptized Christian all over the whole civilized world knew and constantly made use of this famous symbol. It enabled them to recognize each other, for they wore fishes as ornaments or drew them in the dust when they wished to make themselves known to their fellow-believers. A little fish, made sometimes of precious materials, was given to the newly baptized as a *tessera*, to preserve as a memorial of the event and a token of the character he had newly adopted. All that the cross means to Christians of to-day was conveyed to the minds of the faithful of the earliest centuries by the symbol of the fish. For them the use of the cross was impossible, it would at once have betrayed them, but the fish was as full of meaning and at the same time free from all danger.

The fish is one of the most ancient of Christian symbols, and occurs continually both in the Fathers and on Christian monuments. It denotes, primarily, our Lord, and, secondarily, His followers who have become His members by Holy Baptism. Thus Origen speaks of our Lord as figuratively called the Fish, and Tertullian says we are by baptism as little fishes taken out of the water. St. Jerome says that the fish, in which was found the stater of the tribute money, represents Christ who saves all mankind with the price of His blood. Many Fathers comment in a similar strain on the fish of Tobias. Thus St. Prosper of Acquitaine says that " with the interior remedies of this fish we also are illuminated and nourished ".

The fish is often accompanied by some other symbol. Sometimes it swims by a ship, indicating Christ who cares for and watches over the destinies of His Church.

Sometimes it carries the ship on its back, as Christ also sustains His Church. Very frequently it is accompanied by the anchor, which denotes the cross, and then the allusion is to the Crucifixion, or to the sufferings of Christ or of his martyrs. Hence the anchor comes to have the secondary meaning of *hope*, and there is often an inscription which accompanies it, such as *Spes in Christo*—Hope in Christ. The combination of the fish with bread is of very special importance. The primary allusion is no doubt to the Gospel story, to the bread and fishes of the miracle of the four thousand, or to the broiled fish and bread of which our Lord partook after His Resurrection. But the early Christians saw much more in it than this. We shall have to return to the subject in connection with the symbolism of the Holy Eucharist. The allusion has only to be pointed out to commend itself to all. It speaks of the mystic food, which to our senses indeed seems to be but bread, but in reality is nothing less than Christ Himself.

The dolphin in particular was chosen as the fish to be thus represented. It owes its position in this respect to the tradition that it was always the friend and the saviour of men, and this rendered it particularly suitable for the purpose. Sometimes it is transfixed by a trident, and then it represents more particularly the Passion of our Saviour.

Other Symbols.

The other symbols are of far less importance and need not take up much of our space. The ship is always the Church, tossed on the stormy waters of persecution, or sailing calmly over brighter seas. The serpent has several meanings. Sometimes it represents the evil one, in allusion to the fall of man, sometimes the

Redeemer, in allusion to the Brazen Serpent lifted up in the wilderness. Sometimes again the allusion is to those words of our Lord, " Be ye wise as serpents ". It is sometimes also, but rarely, used as a symbol of immortality, its habit of sloughing its skin, and emerging in new and brighter condition being probably the origin. The palm, then as now, was the symbol of martyrdom, but it does not invariably have that meaning. It would not be safe, for instance, to assume that a sepulchral monument which bears the palm upon it is necessarily the tomb of a martyr. Eggs again were a symbol of the Resurrection. Shells of real eggs have been found in early tombs. Here once more the symbolism has lasted on, in the form of Easter eggs, even down to the twentieth century.

We have said enough, without going into any full or scientific discussion of Christian symbolism in these early ages, to show how real and vivid was the language which they spoke. Now that we have mastered the main outlines of that language we are in a position to go on to interrogate the monuments, and to see whether they have any message for us of the faith and doctrine of the Church as held in those first ages when Christians were still so near to the time when our Lord Himself and His Apostles had been among us as teachers of the new and final dispensation. We shall find, if I am not mistaken, that in many details the witness of the monuments fills out and renders clearer than before the evidence of the literary remains of the Christian writers of the period.

CHAPTER II.

The Witness of the Monuments to the Primacy of the Roman See.

THE writings of the Fathers of the first centuries have been ransacked again and again for expressions which may serve to indicate the relations existing in those times between the See of Rome as the heir to the *privilegium Petri* and the rest of the Catholic world. Nor can it be said that the search has failed. Testimonies both clear and numerous have been forthcoming to prove the fact that from the earliest ages the Roman Church and its Bishop were regarded as being in a special way heirs of the commission given by our Lord to St. Peter, and therefore as being specially entitled to the reverence and obedience of Catholic Christendom. These testimonies begin within the Apostolic age, before yet St. John, the last of the Apostles, had passed to his reward, and the first of them is that letter which was written by St. Clement, as Bishop and representative of the Church of Rome, to the disordered and troubled Church of Corinth. This letter is so clear and definite in its statements on this subject that Protestant controversialists, unable to evade its force, have found themselves reduced to speak of it as an instance of the besetting sin of the Roman Church, in always desiring to force her rule upon others, breaking out thus early, in the very first years of her existence. Dr. Salmon speaks of it plainly as the first instance on record of papal aggression. The Church of Corinth, however, were so far from regarding it in this light that they ordered it to be read publicly in the churches side by side with Holy Scripture, in the time of public service.

But over and above these formal documents there is another possible source of evidence on this subject, and indeed on the whole subject of Catholic doctrine, which has up to the present time been left comparatively neglected. This is the evidence of the monuments, and especially of the paintings and inscriptions in the Roman catacombs, some of which may still be seen and read in the very places where they were originally set up ; while others are known to us, although the originals have perished, through the care and labours of archæologists and others who were able to copy them before the injuries of time or of wanton destruction had made it impossible to do so. Every student of Christian antiquities knows the importance of this monumental evidence with regard to the history of Catholic dogma. The detailed statements of the Fathers are borne out and confirmed by these pictures and inscriptions, which were originally inspired by the popular beliefs of the earliest centuries, and sometimes are more eloquent, simple as they are, than the most fervent passages in the writings which they illustrate. They gain a singular power and directness from the very fact that in them controversy is so entirely absent, that there is no thought of persuading the gainsayer or of teaching the ignorant, but that they are the simple and unstudied expression of the thoughts and beliefs which were popularly held in those times and places that now have become so remote to us.

By the nature of the case it is hardly to be expected that there should be very much evidence of this kind bearing upon the question of Roman supremacy. For these inscriptions and paintings are, for the most part, sepulchral in character, and, while we find much that relates to belief in a future life, and to the relations of the living with those who have passed before them into the other world, we cannot reasonably expect to find in such surroundings very clear statements concerning other doctrines, or of matters of government and discipline. We shall have, therefore, to content ourselves in great measure with mere allusions in symbolical language—allusions which, nevertheless, may often afford very valuable testimony concerning the beliefs and feelings of those by whom the representations and inscriptions in question were originally erected.

The Stele of Abercius.

The first piece of documentary evidence on the subject of the Primacy of Rome is, as we have already said, a document sent from Rome to the East, the letter of St. Clement to the Church which was at Corinth. The first piece of monumental evidence available is, on the contrary, a sepulchral monument set up originally in the East, but which after many centuries has found its way to Rome, and may now be seen at the Vatican. It is the famous *Stele* of Abercius, discovered in Phrygia, about thirty years ago, by Professor Ramsay of Aberdeen, and presented to the late Pope Leo XIII on the occasion of his Episcopal Jubilee by the then Sultan of Turkey. It was a singular coincidence which gave to the world almost simultaneously these two long-forgotten testimonies to the Primacy of the Holy See, each in its own class the earliest that we possess—the one, the lost conclusion of the Epistle of St. Clement, found at Constantinople and published by Bryennios, a learned Eastern prelate;

and the other, the *Stele* of Abercius, found in Phrygia and brought to Europe by Professor Ramsay, a member of the Presbyterian Church, and Professor at the University of Aberdeen in Scotland.

Abercius was a priest, perhaps the Bishop of Hieropolis in Phrygia in the latter half of the second century, and was a person of considerable note among the Christians of Asia, standing forth as the champion of Catholicism and unity against the Montanist heresy which had its head-quarters and principal influence in the province of Phrygia. His epitaph, which he wrote in his own lifetime and ordered to be placed upon his tomb, is recorded in his Life, a document given by Symeon Metaphrastes, composed at a much later period, and of little or no value, critical or historical.

It did not at first attract any great attention from scholars, because it was discredited by the surroundings in which it was placed, and regarded by almost all as of very doubtful authenticity. Then came the discovery at Autun, somewhere about the middle of the nineteenth century, of a marble of very early date inscribed with a poem of similar character. This immediately drew the attention of scholars once more to the neglected epitaph of Abercius, and it now seemed to many that it was probably an authentic record which had actually been seen and copied by the writer of the Life some centuries later. It is of course by no means infrequent for genuine records of this kind to be thus incorporated in works that for the most part are worthless as historical material, and a great many valuable scraps of knowledge have been preserved us precisely in this way, and by means of a fortunate accident.

In the year 1881, Professor Ramsay, who was travelling in Phrygia to gather material which might throw new light on the Acts of the Apostles and the missionary journeys of St. Paul, discovered a stone on which were inscribed six verses of the epitaph of Abercius, but with the name, not of Abercius himself but of Alexander. It was evident, however, that this was not the original, for the name of Alexander did not fit the metre, so that the poem could not have been composed for him, but must have been copied and adapted from one that was already in existence. The stone was dated and bore the local year 300, which corresponds to the year 216 of our era. From this discovery two points of the greatest importance were at once established—that the original epitaph and tombstone of Abercius must really have existed, and was not the mere invention of a later century, and that it must have been composed prior to the year 216, which brings us back very nearly to the lifetime of Abercius himself.

But Professor Ramsay's good fortune did not end here. A year or two later, having returned once more to Phrygia, he was able to discover two large fragments of the original inscription itself. One of these he took back with him to Scotland, and the other and larger piece became the property of the Sultan of Turkey, in whose dominions it had been discovered. A little later the Sultan sent his fragment to the Pope, as a present on the occasion of his Episcopal Jubilee, and Professor Ramsay then followed suit by presenting his portion also, so that now the two fragments, once more united, form one of the greatest treasures of the Museum of Christian Antiquities in the Palace of the Lateran.

The poem itself is, of course, written in Greek, and is couched in the highly mystical phraseology, an account of which was given in the last chapter, and which was necessarily adopted by Christians in all similar cases, so long as the fierce persecution of the early

PORTION OF THE STELA OF ABERCIUS

From Cabrol's "Dictionnaire d'Archéologie Chrétienne" (Paris: Letouzey et Ané)

centuries was still in full vigour against them. It is
not easy to give the full force of it in any translation,
but, that we may not be tempted unconsciously to
strain the meaning in a Catholic direction, we can
hardly do better than adopt the one given by the late
Bishop Lightfoot in his "Apostolic Fathers" (Vol. I,
Part II, p. 480) :—

"The citizen of a notable city, I made this tomb in
my lifetime ; that in due season I might have here a
resting-place for my body. Abercius by name, I am
a disciple of the pure Shepherd, who feedeth his flocks
on mountains and plains, who hath great eyes looking
on all sides ; for he taught me faithful writings. He
also sent me to royal Rome to behold it and to see
the golden-robed, golden-slippered Queen. And there
I saw a people bearing a splendid seal. And I saw
the Plain of Syria and all the cities, even Nisibis,
crossing over the Euphrates. And everywhere I had
associates. In company with Paul I followed, while
everywhere Faith led the way, and set before me for
food the fish from the fountain, mighty and stainless
(whom a pure virgin grasped), and gave this to friends
to eat always, having good wine and giving the mixed
cup with bread. These words I, Abercius, standing
by, ordered to be inscribed. In sooth I was in the
course of my seventy-second year. Let every friend
who observeth this pray for me. But no man shall
place another tomb above mine. If otherwise, then he
shall pay two thousand pieces of gold to the treasury
of the Romans and a thousand pieces of gold to my
good fatherland Hieropolis."

The concluding words of this epitaph may, for our
present purpose, be neglected. But the part which
immediately precedes is, assuredly, by no means
unimportant. It tells, in language which, if always
intentionally mystical and veiled, would yet have been

quite sufficient to convey a clear meaning to anyone who was accustomed to this manner of speaking, about the principal doctrines and practices of the Catholic Church. To a Catholic even of to-day the words seem so definite and plain that it is very hard for him to understand that there are many who want to deny that the inscription is even Christian. Abercius is recording on his tomb the main features of his faith in order that his fellow-believers may read it and understand and so be moved to utter a prayer for the well-being of his soul. He tells us, therefore, of the Good Shepherd whose disciple he is, whose flock is but one over all the world, in Phrygia as well as everywhere else. He tells how the Shepherd is Himself sinless, and that His glance penetrates everywhere so that nothing can be hidden from His knowledge. He speaks of the universality of Catholicism, as opposed to the local character of Montanism : " everywhere he had found fellow-worshippers ". Faith had been his guide, and the writings of St. Paul were in his hands —his constant companion on his journey. Then, in words the importance of which can scarcely be over-estimated, he speaks of the Holy Eucharist ; the food by which he had been sustained as he travelled. It is Faith again who gives him to eat and the food is the mystical Fish, the incarnate God, born of the pure virgin. There, too, is bread and the mingled chalice.

The passage is most important, and we shall have to return to it again, as an evidence of the clear belief of the second century in the doctrine of the Real Presence in the Holy Eucharist, as also in the doctrine of late years brought into discussion, of the Virgin birth of our Blessed Lord. It is important also as witnessing to the fountain of baptism as the only way in which access can be gained to the presence of our Lord in the Holy Eucharist. But before Abercius comes to speak of these doctrines he deals with another, and one which was in his eyes of particular importance, since it was just then especially assaulted in Phrygia. It is the doctrine of the Unity of the Church and the Primacy of the Roman Pontiff. The Good Shepherd, who is his Master, "sends him to Royal Rome that he may see it," or as others prefer to read the passage, "sends him to Rome that he may behold a King" or "a Kingdom". The style of the whole epitaph demands a mystic interpretation here also, just as in the case of the Shepherd, the Fish or the Fountain. It is impossible, therefore, to interpret it of the Roman Empire or of the reigning Emperor. Why should the Good Shepherd desire His servant to study the secular Empire? The whole poem was intended to be, in the words of Professor Ramsay, "the imperishable record, amid the most solemn and impressive surroundings, of the testimony of Abercius in favour of the one and indivisible Church Catholic, and against the separation and the nationalism of Montanus". The "Kingdom" then, if that be the true reading, must naturally be interpreted of the Church, the Kingdom of God upon earth, over which the Good Shepherd Himself was reigning as Emperor. Every Christian who was familiar with the Gospels would at once have grasped the allusion. Nor is the interpretation more difficult of "the Queen with golden robes and wearing golden shoes". It is the Church of Christ again, under the aspect of the Bride, and the imagery is derived from the words of the Psalmist: *Astitit regina a dextris tuis, in vestitu deaurato, circumdata varietatibus.* It seems impossible to escape from this conclusion, and indeed no other plausible interpretation has ever been put forward by those who accept the epitaph as being really a Christian monument, though many, with Lightfoot and Ramsay among them, have been content to pass over the subject with but slight discussion and almost in silence.

But if this conclusion once be granted, how tremendously important is the reference to Rome. In the mind of this Eastern bishop of the second century, if a man wishes to study the Church of Christ in her aspect as a Queen ; if he would familiarize himself with the working of the Kingdom of God upon earth, it is not in Phrygia or in any provincial city that he can satisfy his ambition. No, he must go to Rome, and go in the spirit of a disciple, and taking Faith as his guide ; and there in Rome, and in Rome alone, will he find what he wants to examine. It was precisely because Rome was the centre and the capital of Christendom, the throne upon earth of that mystical Queen in the raiment of gold, because, in a word, "Rome had always held the primacy," and other Churches were bound to agree with her *propter potiorem principalitatem*, as St. Irenaeus was saying almost at the same moment that the Good Shepherd willed His disciple to come thither, as a humble learner wearing the garb of a pilgrim. A great deal has been written on this epitaph of Abercius, as was, of course, inevitable in the case of so important a monument ; and every endeavour has been made to interpret it in any other than a Christian and Catholic manner. But in spite of all such endeavours, no other interpretation has as yet been suggested which is not obviously far-fetched and improbable. It remains, therefore, a most valuable witness to second-century belief on these great doctrines of the Church, and its consequent value and importance can hardly be placed at too high a level.[1]

[1] Those who desire to study this subject may consult the following: Pitra in " Spicil. Solesm.," iii. 532 ; De Rossi, " Inscr. Christ.," ii. 1 ; G. Ficker in the " Sitzungsberichte " of the Academy of Berlin, 1894 ; Duchesne in the " Bulletin Critique," 1894 ; De Rossi, " Bollett. d' arch. crist.," 1894 ; Marucchi, " Nuovo Bull. d' arch. crist.," 1895 ;

Representations of the Apostles.

Our next piece of evidence comes from a period slightly later indeed than that with which we have so far been dealing, but still often well within the ages of persecution. It consists of a number of representations of the Apostles St. Peter and St. Paul which have been found painted on the walls of the catacombs, engraved on gems or on glass, or carved on sarcophagi of the third and fourth centuries. These representations are in almost every case strictly conformed to a certain type of feature in their presentment of the two great Apostles, and there is every reason to believe that in them we have traditionally handed down to us the actual portraits of those to whom Christian Rome owed so much, and who were always, from the earliest times, regarded as her founders and patrons. Even when all the Apostles are represented it is noticeable that these two are marked off from the rest, and given a place of honour and precedence. Sometimes they are seated while all the rest stand ; or sometimes, in the late compositions, they are distinguished from the others by means of the circular nimbus. But what is especially interesting from our present point of view is that, while these two are thus uniformly distinguished above the rest, they are not represented as equal in dignity between themselves, but there is always a further distinction by which St. Peter is given a rank superior to his brother

Harnack in " Texte und Untersuchungen," 1895 ; Duchesne, " Mélanges d'arch. et d'histoire," xv. ; Zahn, " Neue Kirchliche Zeitschrift," 1895 ; " Analecta Bollandiana," 1897 ; " Bessarione," 1898 ; De Sanctis in " Zeitschrift für Katholische Theologie," 1897 ; and especially " Declerq in Dict.".

Among English writers the following should be consulted : Ramsay, "Journal of Hellenic Studies," 1882 and 1883 ; Lightfoot, " Colossians," p. 54, and " Apostolic Fathers," Vol. I, Part II, p. 472 *seq.*, and in the " Expositor," 1885 ; Ramsay, " Expositor," 1889.

Apostle. It is not merely that he is on the right of our Lord while St. Paul is on the left. To that rule there are several exceptions, and it is never safe to draw any conclusion of this sort as to the relative precedence of right and left in any monument which is earlier than the mediæval period. The question was finally decided in favour of the dexter side only by the rise of the science of heraldry.

The mark which most frequently distinguishes St. Peter in the earliest representations is that our Lord is depicted in the act of handing to him a roll or a volume, an act which is sometimes explained by the accompanying inscription, DOMINUS LEGEM DAT. Of this class of representation a good many instances have come down to us. The most famous is, perhaps, the well-known sarcophagus which came originally from the Vatican Cemetery, and is now in the Museum of Christian Antiquities at the Lateran. On this sarcophagus Christ is shown already ascended into Heaven, but handing over to St. Peter, as his visible representative upon earth, the volume of the Law of the New Dispensation. There is a painting of the same subject in the Catacomb of St. Priscilla ; and on a gilded glass, now in the Vatican Museum, the volume actually bears the title, LEX DOMINI. Most important of all this class, perhaps, is the mosaic in Sta Costanze on the Via Salaria, where the whole parallel is carefully worked out between the giving of the Law of the Old Covenant to Moses on Mount Sinai and the giving of the New Law to Peter the Apostle. From it we see at once what was the real thought underlying all these representations. All that Moses was to the Jews—the Chosen Lawgiver appointed by God, whom it was their duty to obey and to follow—all that, and more than that, St. Peter was to be in the Christian communion. He is the Moses

CHRIST GIVES THE LAW TO ST. PETER

From a sarcophagus in the Lateran Museum

From Marucchi's "I Monumenti del Museo Cristiano Pio-Lateranense"
(Milan : Ulrico Hoepli)

St. Peter as Moses and Arrest of St. Peter

From a sarcophagus in the Lateran Museum

From Marucchi's "I Monumenti del Museo Cristiano Pio-Lateranense" (Milan : Ulrico Hoepli)

of the New Covenant, the Lawgiver and Leader of the Catholic Church of Christ, specially sent and commissioned that he may bring the people of God through the wilderness of earthly life to the Land of Promise, the spiritual Canaan. No image could possibly have been chosen which would express more fully and conclusively the whole doctrine of the Supremacy of Peter and of his successors in the Pontifical office.

The giving of the Law on Sinai is not the only incident in the life of Moses which finds frequent representation in the monuments of the earliest centuries. Another attitude in which he is often depicted is striking the rock and causing the water to flow forth for the relief of the thirsty multitude. This representation, again, like all those which are found in the catacombs, must not be taken as merely historical, but as conveying a second and mystical interpretation drawn from the words of St. Paul : " And they drank of the Rock that followed them, and that Rock was Christ" (1 Cor. x. 4). Moses is the representative, that is, of the authority of the Church, who draws forth from the Rock the living stream of Divine grace for the nourishing and refreshment of the souls of her children. Here, again, it is interesting to note that St. Peter was regarded as the authority in the Church of whom the type in the older Covenant had been presented by Moses. It is not only that the features of the Lawgiver as he strikes the rock are generally those which every Roman Christian knew and recognized at once as those of the Prince of the Apostles, but that the actual name of Peter is not infrequently inscribed, especially in the gilded glasses of the third and fourth centuries, as if to ensure that the application should always be realized. There are two well-known examples in the Vatican Library, in each of which the inscription consists only of the name of PETROS. A still more notable example, which we have already quoted in another connection,[1] is to be found in the well-known dish, found originally at Podgoritza in Dalmatia, but

VASE FOUND AT PODGORITZA.
(*From Marucchi's " Eléments d'Archæologie," Descle De Brouwer et Cie.*)

now in the collection of M. Basilewski at Paris, on which the inscription is given in full, PETROS VIRGA PERQVODSET FONTES CIPERVNT QVORERE—Peter

[1] *Supra*, p. 83.

struck with his rod, the fountains began to flow. Analogous again to these is a glass which is now preserved in the British Museum, on which is represented the Chair of Peter, surmounted by the monogram of Christ. It has in the background the rock, from which water is flowing, and on the top of the rock rises the Christian altar. The whole might well serve as an illustration of the words of Pope Innocent I to the Fathers of Africa, when he spoke of the Chair of Peter as being the source "whence all waters issue and flow through all the regions of the world as pure streams from a spotless fountain (Constant., "Epist. Rom. Pont.," p. 801).

The Good Shepherd.

Another class of representations must next engage our attention. No figure is more frequent or more characteristic of the art of the catacombs than that of our Blessed Lord in the character of the Good Shepherd. He is commonly represented as a beardless youth bearing a lamb upon his shoulders. But sometimes, as notably in the case of an ancient statue found in the course of the excavating the lower church of S. Clemente at Rome, the same attitude was adopted for the statues of St. Peter, the Shepherd to whom Christ assigned His flock, and who was charged with the duty of feeding the sheep and guiding the flock in the place of his Master. Another important monument which sets forth the same idea in a slightly different manner may be found in a sarcophagus which is one of the most beautiful and interesting of those preserved in the Lateran collection. Christ, wearing the dress of a shepherd, and carrying the shepherd's staff in His hands, stands in the midst of the Apostles, all similarly habited as shepherds, and each one having in front of him a sheep to represent the portion of the

flock committed to his charge. On the right of our
Lord stands St. Peter, and St. Paul in the corresponding place on His left. The general subject of the
design is evidently the Shepherd of shepherds in the
midst of those to whom collectively He has assigned
the care of His flock. But He turns especially towards St. Peter, and lays His hand as if in benediction
upon the sheep that belongs to him and stands immediately before him. It brings back irresistibly to
the mind the words once spoken so solemnly to that
Apostle : " Feed My sheep," and seems to repeat to
us the truth that the flock of Peter is in a special way
the flock of Christ, and that Peter, more than the other
Apostles, is charged with the care of all and general
superintendence.[1]

Papal Sepulchres.

The places of burial selected for the earliest Popes
are worth a moment's consideration in this connection.
It is manifest that they were generally considered to
hold a relation to St. Peter, which was quite other
than that in which they stood to St. Paul. The
earliest bishops of Rome were buried on the Vatican
close round the tomb which contained the relics of
the Apostle. There their bodies were found, in the
excavations in 1626, still largely preserved by the
quasi-embalming process to which they had been subjected, and surrounding St. Peter like bishops attend-
ing a council.[2] When no more space was available
at the Vatican, the next series of Pontiffs, from Pope
St. Zephyrinus onwards in A.D. 220, were laid in the
so-called Papal Crypt, in the Catacomb of St. Callixtus,
since that cemetery had now become the official property of the Church. When this very fact led to its

[1] See plate opposite p. 166.
[2] Barnes, " St. Peter in Rome," p. 323.

confiscation under Galerius in 258, a new burying-place had to be chosen. This was selected in the cemetery of St. Priscilla, the oldest of all the cemeteries of the Church, but still protected by the right of private property. The point of the selection was that here again there were Petrine memories. It was the place *ubi Petrus baptizaverat*, where his chair had been placed and whence tradition told that he had governed the Church. If they could not lie close to his relics on the Vatican, there was no more appropriate spot to be found for the burial of those who had succeeded him in the exercise of apostolic authority. But never was any Pope in those earliest centuries laid to rest where the *trophæum* of St. Paul on the Ostian Way was visited by the pilgrims who found their way to the eternal city.

Other Inscriptions.

We turn lastly to the inscriptions of the early centuries to ask whether they have any further light to shed upon the matter. It must be admitted that, as regards the inscriptions of the earliest centuries—of all the inscriptions, that is—which date from the times of persecution, there is little or nothing to be gathered germane to our present inquiry. The sepulchral inscriptions of this period which mark out the tombs of the Pontiffs are remarkable chiefly for their brevity and simplicity. CORNELIVS MARTYR EP may stand as a specimen of the later ones, while the earliest of all are exactly of the same character and only differ by being inscribed in Greek characters. The title of *Papa* is given to a Patriarch of Alexandria at an earlier date than, as far as we know, it was applied to the Bishop of Rome; and that of *Pontifex Maximus* is of much later date, and even to the present day is never employed in any ecclesiastical document. The stone which closed in the sepulchral vault of St. Paul, and which to this day may be seen under the High Altar of his church, is of Constantinian date, but is inscribed simply with the three words PAULO APOSTOLO MARTYRI. There must have been some such inscription in earlier days both over his tomb and over that of St. Peter, for we learn from Eusebius that in his day there were "monuments of Peter and Paul, distinguished by name, even now visible in the cemeteries of Rome". But we have no ground whatever for supposing that the inscription at the tomb of St. Peter made any reference to his position as the Vicar of Christ or as Chief Pastor of the Catholic Church. An inscription in Greek characters is most probable, altogether similar to that which Constantine put—or was it renewed?—above the body of St. Paul, PETRO APOSTOLO MARTYRI.

But so soon as peace had been given to the Church, and Christians were free to express themselves openly on the subject of their belief, we do meet with inscriptions which set forth the position of St. Peter and of his successors as the possessors in the Church of a primacy of jurisdiction. In the inscription which Constantine set up over the great arch of the Basilica of St. Peter, the old symbolism of the catacombs is clearly referred to, and the Apostle is set forth to us as the Moses of the New Covenant, leading his people victoriously to a better land.

QVOD DVCE TE MVNDVS SVRREXIT IN ASTRA
    TRIVMPHANS
HANC CONSTANTINVS VICTOR TIBI CONDIDIT
    AULAM.

" Because under thy guidance the world rose triumphing to the stars, therefore the victorious Constantine has built for thee this church."

A little later came St. Damasus, who did so ad-

TOMBSTONE (FOURTH CENTURY) OF ST. PAUL THE APOSTLE

mirable a work in preserving for future generations the
various sites which tradition had handed down as
connected with the great events of Catholic history.
Several of his inscriptions have reference to St. Peter,
and set forth his position in no ambiguous language.
At the Platonia in the Catacomb of St. Sebastian—
the place where the bodies of the Apostles once rested
—the inscription claims them both as Roman citizens:
ROMA SVOS POTIUS MERVIT DEFENDERE CIVES.
In the Baptistery at St. Peter's he went further, and
definitely claimed for St. Peter the primacy and the
right by Divine appointment of being the centre of
unity:—

SED PRAESTANTE PETRO CVI TRADITA IANVA
    COELI EST
ANTISTES CHRISTI COMPOSVIT DAMASVS
VNA PETRI SEDES, VNVM VERVMQUE LAVACRVM
    VINCVLA NVLLA TENENT QVEM LIQVOR ISTE
    LAVAT.

Two other inscriptions which still remain at Rome
are specially important as setting forth the primacy of
jurisdiction of St. Peter's successors. The first was
found at Sta Pudenziana, and is contemporary with
Pope Siricius, who reigned from 384 to 398, and to
whom it refers:—

SALVO SIRICIO EPISCOPO SANCTAE ECCLESIAE.

The other is still *in situ* over the great door of the
Basilica of Sta Sabina, inside the church. It is of the
date of the Council of Ephesus, and refers to that
Pope St. Celestine (A.D. 422-432) whose legates pre-
sided at that Council, and is therefore of very special
importance:—

CVLMEN APOSTOLICVM CVM CAELESTINVS HA-
    BERET
PRIMVS ET IN TOTO FVLGERET EPISCOPVS ORBE

—When Celestine held the Apostolic height, and shone as first bishop over the whole world.

It is the last piece of evidence we shall quote, and surely leaves nothing to be desired on the score of completeness or of clear definition.

CHAPTER III.

The Witness of the Monuments with Regard to Holy Baptism.

BAPTISM in the early centuries (when it was not a case of the children of Christian parents, who, as Tertullian says, do not become Christians, but are born so) was always preceded by a period of instruction which was called the Catechumenate. There was a certain ceremony in admitting inquirers to this grade, consisting generally in prayer with the imposition of hands. Thus in the life of St. Martin by Severus Sulpitius (" Dial.," ii. cap. v.) we read that that saint was accustomed to admit postulants to the Catechumenate wherever he might be, even in the open fields, by laying his hand on each of them. Some of the ancient liturgical books have a rite appointed for this purpose, under the title " Ad Christianum faciendum ".

This Catechumenate lasted for a considerable period. In the second and third centuries it was extended generally to three years, and this period is laid down in the " Apostolical Constitutions " (viii. c. 32), with the proviso, however, that it might be shortened in special cases. If a catechumen fell seriously ill during this period, and was in danger of death, he was at once baptized. St. Basil, for instance (" Epist.," 176), writes to the wife of Arintheus, a Roman prætor, saying that he baptized him although only a catechumen, because he was in danger of dying.

There were various grades in the Catechumenate. The *audientes*, or *hearers*, were admitted to the church to hear the lessons from Holy Scripture and the Homily, but to nothing else. It was for these that St. Augustine wrote his work, " De catechizandis rudibus," and we can gather from that book how far their instruction had to go before they were admitted to the next grade, that of the *Genuflectentes*, or kneelers. These were admitted to the prayers and received the blessing of the Bishop. There was a special place in the Mass beyond which they might not stay, and the earlier portion of the Liturgy hence acquired the name of *Missa Cate-chumenorum*. Lastly, there were the *Competentes* who were ready and anxious for the Sacrament, and to these, at last, was taught the mystery of the Holy Trinity and the Sacrament of Penance.

Baptism was usually conferred on converts only on one or at most on two occasions in the year, on Holy Saturday and the Eve of Pentecost. The whole of Lent was in some sort a special preparation, and was fasted rigorously by those who were candidates. The new name, the Christian name as we still say, the imposition of which was held to imply the acceptance of Christian obligations, was given on the fourth Sunday of Lent in the West (Aug. " Serm.," ccxiii.), and on the second Sunday in the East (Cyril., " Hier. Catech.," iii.). It marked yet another stage in the long preparation. The next step was the confession of sins made to the Bishop, which took place about Passion Sunday, and was followed by the *Scrutiny*, a ceremony which lasted for seven days. On each day the catechumens came to the church, bareheaded and barefooted, and took their stand in the appointed place. Then came the exorcists and did their office. They blew three times in the face of each, and then touched their nostrils and ears with saliva, while they recited over them the prayers of exorcism. By the sixth century there had been added the ceremony of placing salt in their mouths, and this was then considered an ancient ceremony going back to the Apostles. So it may have been introduced long before, although we have no trace of it (Isid. Hisp., "De div. off.," ii. 20 ; Aug., "De nupt. et concup.," II. xxix. 50).

Such was the Catechumenate in early times. There are many inscriptions commemorating catechumens in the catacombs. Here it may suffice to note one only, which may yet be seen in the Vigna Vannutelli on the Via Tiburtina, fixed to the wall of the Osteria in the place of the bowling-green.

ΚΙΤΕ · ΒΙΚΤΟΡ · ΚΑΤΗΧΟΥΜΕΝΟC
ΑΙΤΩΝ · ΕΙΚΟCΙ · ΠΑΡΘΕΝΟC
ΔΟΥΛΟC · ΤΟΥ · ΚΥΡΙΟΥ · ΙΗCΟΥ ☧

Here lies Victor, a Catechumen, aged twenty years.
A Servant of the Lord Jesus Christ.

The Method of Baptizing.

If we are to trust the references to the administration of baptism which are to be found in the pages of the Fathers, we shall almost certainly be led to the conclusion that the sacrament was always given, in the case of adults no less than of little children, by the method of complete submersion, the whole body of the candidate being plunged under the water, so as to be entirely submerged at one and the same moment. No doubt this was what was generally regarded as ideal, and it is only thus that the full force of St. Paul's words, "Buried with Him in baptism," could be realized. But, in practice, although such immersion

8

of infants caused little difficulty, it was scarcely possible to arrange for it in the case of grown men and women. A great depth of water would be required, and this, especially in the times of persecution, would be very hard to obtain. St. Peter himself is said to have baptized in the Tiber, though the evidence for this is not very strong. Still, it may have been possible for him to do so in the earliest years, before the outbreak of the first great persecution of Nero. After that date it would have been quite impossible.

It is at this point that the evidence of the monuments becomes valuable, as supplementing and ex-

BAPTISM OF CHRIST, from
the Crypt of Lucina.

BAPTISM, in the Gallery
of the Sacraments, in
the Catacomb of St.
Callixtus.

(*From Rogers' " Baptism and Christian Archæology," Oxford University Press.*)

plaining the evidence of the Fathers. We have in the paintings of the catacombs a great number of representations of the act of baptism ; some depicting the Christian sacrament and others the baptism of Christ. Both are valuable evidence for our purpose, for there is no reason to doubt that each alike would represent the ceremony as it was ordinarily administered, so that it might at once be recognized by the faithful who looked upon it.

The earliest representation of all is in the Crypt of Lucina on the Appian Way, which now forms part of the Catacomb of St. Callixtus. It dates from the first century or at latest from the beginning of the second. The scene is that of the baptism of Christ. The Baptist stands on the right and holds out his hand to a nude figure moving towards him as if it came out of the water. The dove is seen on the left of the picture. The water has disappeared through age, but could not have been depicted, from the relative position of the figures, as rising higher than to our Lord's knees, as the Baptist is apparently standing on dry ground.

Of even greater importance for our present purpose are two pictures in the so-called Gallery of the Sacraments in the Catacomb of St. Callixtus. These again are of very early date, somewhere about the year A.D. 200.

In the first the baptizer stands on dry ground to the left of the picture. He is clothed in a white toga and lays his right hand on the head of the catechumen, who is represented as a nude boy. The water rises to the ankles.

In the second picture the baptizer stands on the right and has a cloth round his loins. The catechumen is again a nude boy. Both are standing in the water, which just covers the ankles, and the baptizer is in the act of pouring water over the head of the boy. The falling water is represented by six large strokes of dark blue paint.

BAPTISM, in the Gallery of the Sacraments, in the Catacomb of St. Callixtus.

These three are the three oldest representations of baptism which we possess, and their evidence is of the highest importance, especially as it is entirely borne out

8 *

and confirmed by a mass of later representations.[1] The points worthy of notice are these. In every case the baptizer is clothed. It was not then customary for him in these early times to go down into deep water with the candidate, but he stood on dry land, or at most went into shallow water. Otherwise he would have removed his clothes. The candidate is in every case completely naked, for, although the water is not shown as deep enough for submersion, it was held right that the bathing should be complete and involve every portion of the body. This was effected, since it was not ordinarily possible to do it in any other way, by means of affusion, pouring water from a vessel over the head.

That this was the ordinary way in which baptism was given to adults in the ages of persecution is made clear to us again by the evidence of the baptisteries or places where the sacrament was administered. At first any running water was utilized for the purpose, as we see in the story of the baptism of the eunuch by St. Philip; but very soon, as the ritual became more settled, it became usual to administer the sacrament within doors and usually in a special place appointed for the purpose. In those cases when the sacrament was given, as we know was not unusual, in private houses, total submersion would have been impossible, and some such method as that which is depicted in the catacombs must have been followed, for want of a bath sufficiently large and deep to make submersion possible. Thus in the Acts of St. Lawrence (Surius, "Vit. Sanct.," Aug. 10, § 16) the Saint is said to have baptized Lucillus, a fellow-prisoner. "He blessed the water, and, when he had undressed him, he poured the water over his head saying. . . ." So again in the story of the boy Athanasius baptizing

---

[1] See, for instance, the sarcophagus from the Lateran Museum, on plate opposite p. 148.

his playmates on the seashore : he did it by pouring water over them, not by immersing them in the sea (Rufinus, " H.E.," i. 14). That this method was the only one possible in the case of clinical baptisms is also obvious.

Baptisteries.

It was, however, soon felt that, although the practice of baptizing in private houses was, of course, perfectly valid, and, under the circumstances of the persecution, very excusable, yet the dignity of the sacrament demanded a fixed and settled place for its administration. Such places may have existed in some of the great private houses, but we have no certain tradition on the subject, and the evidence seems to tend in the opposite direction. In the catacombs, however, there were undoubtedly such places. Boldetti speaks of several as existing in his days, but only three are known at the present time.

The earliest of these is the one discovered by Professor Marucchi in the cemetery of St. Priscilla in 1901, and by him identified with the place *ad nymphas ubi Petrus baptizavit*, though others regard it as only of the fourth century. The basin can hardly have been used for immersion, and the sacrament was almost certainly administered by affusion. The niches for the lamps are round the chapel and leave the tank below in darkness.[1]

The second is in the Cœmeterium Ostrianum, close to Sta Agnese, and was discovered in 1876. It seems to be of the third century. The water flows into a hollow cut in the rock which is neither large nor deep, though exact measurements have not been published.

In the cemetery of Pontianus is another, apparently

---

[1] " Bull. d' arch. crist.," 1901, with plan and photographs.

of the sixth century. The tank is about 3 feet deep but is seldom full. There is an important fresco of the baptism of our Lord above it.

By the end of the fourth century there were already regular baptisteries erected in connection with the principal churches. By far the greater number of baptisms at this period must have been those of the infant children of Christian parents, but paganism was still strong, and there must also have been constant need for a font large enough to allow of the baptism by immersion of adult converts. It becomes, therefore, distinctly interesting to ascertain what was the size and especially the depth of these fonts, in order to discover the nature of the ceremony employed; whether, in short, complete submersion was considered necessary, or whether the usual practice after the peace of the church, continued identical with that which we have shown to have been usual during the centuries of persecution. Now the first of all these baptisteries, and by far the most important of all, inasmuch as it sets the norm, which all other and later baptisteries tend to follow, was, of course, the great round baptistery at the Lateran which was built by Constantine and still remains. The basin is octagonal and the depth about 3 feet. Its size is quite abnormal, as befits the font of the Cathedral Church of Rome.

This depth of about 3 feet seems to be almost general in the baptismal fonts of the fourth and fifth centuries, so far as we can now recover the facts. It was thus in the font at S. Stefano on the Via Latina,[1] as we can see, although the font itself is almost destroyed, by the fact that the holes for filling and for emptying the tank still remain visible. It is circular in shape and about 6 feet in diameter. So, again, at Naples, in

---

[1] Marucchi, " Éléments d'arch. chré.," ii. p. 200.

the baptistery which was once attached to the Church of Sta Restituta, and still more clearly at the Catacombs of St. Januarius, there are remains of fonts of the fourth century, the size and depth of which were almost identical with that at S. Stefano.

Outside of Italy there still exist some ancient fonts of this period. In Egypt there is one at the White Monastery (Dair al Abiad), near Abydos. It is about 4 feet across and 3 feet in depth. In Syria there is one at Tyre discovered in 1874 by Dr. Sepp.[1] It is $2\frac{1}{2}$ feet in depth and seems to be the original font built by Paulinus in 314. Another was discovered at Amwas in 1884 by Dr. Schick.[2] Here the water could never have been more that 2 feet in depth, and the depth would seem to have been even less in the instance at Beit' Aûwa, near Hebron, which is described by Conder.[3] Altogether, the evidence of the baptisteries seems perfectly clear, and entirely in accordance with that of the pictures of the catacombs. Children may have continued to be baptized by total immersion until a comparatively late period, but for adults it can never have been practicable. Everywhere in the earliest ages the practice would seem to have been invariable. The baptizer, bishop, and priest, stood at the side of the font and did not go down into the water. The candidate for baptism, apparently always at this time completely undressed, stood in the shallow water and was baptized, thus standing, by a triple affusion poured upon his head and flowing over the whole body. In later times the affusion over the head came to be considered all that was necessary, and as it was not now thought needful that the

---

[1] " Meerfahrt nach Tyrus " (Leipzig, 1879), p. 217.
[2] " Zeitschrift d. Deutsch Palästina Vereins," 1884, p. 15.
[3] Conder and Kitchener, " Survey of Western Palestine," 1883, p. 321.

whole body should be wetted, there was no longer any reason why the clothes should be removed.

The Doctrine of Holy Baptism.

So far we have considered nothing except the manner in which the sacrament was conferred in the earliest times. We have learnt that some of the ceremonies which we now associate with baptism itself—the insufflation, the touching with saliva, the placing salt in the mouth—were originally connected with the catechumenate rather than with the sacrament, although others, such as the lighting of a candle, the clothing in a white robe, and so forth, are actually connected with baptism, and have a very obvious symbolism. But it is not only upon the ceremonies of baptism that the monuments have a message to give us. They speak to us also of doctrine, and by interpreting the symbolism of the representations of which we have spoken we can learn much of the belief of those first ages as to the meaning and efficacy of the sacrament.

The symbolical representations are of two kinds. The first kind concerns itself with the striking of the rock by Moses, and the second with the general symbolism of the fish.

The figure of Moses never bears the horns of light with which we are familiar in later representations, but generally is given the well-known features of the Apostle St. Peter, the actual name of Peter being added in several instances later than the peace of the Church. The meaning of these pictures, therefore, was, that as Moses, the lawgiver of the Old Covenant, brought water from the rock for the refreshment of Israel, so also does Peter, the lawgiver of the New Covenant, and those who act with him and derive

MOSES STRIKING THE ROCK

From a sarcophagus in the Lateran Museum

From Marucchi's " I Monumenti del Museo Cristiano Pio-Lateranense"
(Milan : Ulrico Hoepli)

their authority from him, draw from the side of Christ, who is typified by the Rock, the sacrament of baptism for the remission of sins. "This is the water," says Tertullian ("De bapt.," 9), "which from the Rock flowed down to the people." "The Rock was smitten," says St. Augustine ("Serm.," 352), "that grace might be able to approach us."

In some of these pictures of Moses and the rock we may see the application driven home by the presence of one of the faithful with his head under the stream which gushes from the place where the rod has struck. He is not trying to drink, which shows that the symbolism is not connected with the other sacrament of the Holy Eucharist, but gives himself up to the cleansing and refreshment supplied by the mystic stream. It is another argument for the practice, for which we have already contended, of baptism by affusion in those times.

The symbolism of the fish is well drawn out by Tertullian. "Our Lord Himself," he tells us, "is the great Fish, the true Ichthus—*Sed nos pisciculi secundum Piscem nostrum Jesum Christum*—but we are little fishes also, sharing in His nature" ("De bapt.," c. i. ; Migne, "P.L.," i. 1198). The Apostles and their successors are the fishermen, according to the promise of Christ, "I will make you fishers of men" (Matt. IV. 19), and they draw us out of the water with the hook of the sacrament. The hook, rather than the net, is chosen for this symbolism because the sacraments are administered to individuals, and we enter into the Kingdom of God one by one rather than as members of a crowd. In the Chapel of the Sacraments at St. Callixtus, in the same picture as one of those to which we have already alluded as showing the act of baptism, may be seen a fisherman seated on a rock and drawing out a little fish from the water in this manner.

Many are the scenes from the Old Testament which were enlisted in the same way to teach to the faithful the mystery of baptism. We find them everywhere in the catacombs, and their meaning is explained to us by many a passage from contemporary Fathers. Noe and the ark is of course obvious in this connection, and its use is very ancient, since we find it already in the so-called Greek Chapel at Sta Priscilla, which dates from the second century. So again the passage of the Red Sea (cf. 1 Cor. x. 2) or of the Jordan, suggested the passage from the darkness of idolatry to the knowledge of the Divine law. St. Chrysostom (*In dictum Pauli, Nolo vos ignorari*, Migne, "P.G.," li. 247) explains the symbolism at great length. For St. Hippolytus, Susannah is the great type of baptism. The day when she went to bathe, he says, prefigured the Pascal feast when in the garden of the church the bath is prepared for the catechumens burning with desire. The elders represent the powers of evil from which escape is made through holy baptism (in Dan. i. 16; cf. Cyril Hier., "Catech.," iii. 5). The application explains to us the reason why the story of Susannah and the elders was one of those most frequently depicted on the walls of the catacombs.

The inscriptions come to the aid of the pictures, though, naturally, they are less definite and instructive. An instance found at Aquileia incised on marble gives a representation of the baptism of a young girl with the inscription inNOCENTI SPiritO QVEM ELEGIT DOMinus PAVSAT IN PACE FIDELIS. It is noteworthy for two reasons. The first is the vessel over the neophyte's head, from which the water pours down upon her. The second is the absolute nudity of the recipient, in spite of her sex. It shows that the custom of giving over the details of the baptism of persons of her sex to deaconesses was not general or invariable,[1] and we recall the words of St. Augustine : "Naked are we born into the world, naked also we come to the font ; so that naked and unburdened we may hasten to the gate of heaven. How foolish is it and incongruous that one whom his mother bore naked, whom the Church again received naked, should desire to enter heaven possessing riches" ("Serm.," xx.).

Ceremonies connected with Baptism.

In the earliest times on the third day of the Scrutiny, but later on immediately before the actual baptism, came the initiation of the catechumen into a further knowledge of Christian doctrine. Not even yet was the doctrine of the Holy Eucharist communicated, but a further step forward was made. Certain pages from the Gospels were read, the Creed was recited for the first time, and, most important of all, the *Paternoster*, the prayer of the faithful, which might not be said by any but the initiated, was now pronounced and taught. Mgr. Duchesne in his "Origines du Culte Chrétien," thinks that we have a representation of this initiation in the well-known scene of the giving of the law to Moses, here again represented generally with the features and sometimes with the name of Peter, which is so frequent in Christian paintings and sculptures of the period. "Christ is there depicted as seated on a splendid throne placed on the summit of a mountain from whence flow the four rivers of Paradise. Around him are assembled the Apostles. St. Peter, their chief, receives from the hands of the Saviour a book—emblem of the Christian Law—on which is inscribed DOMINVS LEGEM DAT or some similar device. Above this group there appear in the azure of the sky the

---

[1] "Const. Ap.," iii. 15, 16.

four symbolical animals with the four books of the
Gospel. I would not take upon myself to say that this
scene was expressly depicted from the ritual of the
'Traditio Legis Christi,' but there is such a striking
resemblance between the two things, that the likeness
could not fail to have been remarked. Many of the
faithful when casting their eyes upon the paintings
which decorated the apses of their churches, must have
had thus brought before them one of the most beautiful ceremonies of their initiation." [1]

Infant Baptism.

Actual infants were, of course, baptized from the first
years of Christianity. We know this from the Fathers,
but the monuments are equally decisive on the point.
Thus Marini ("Arvali," p. 171) has preserved for us
an inscription which commemorates the burial of a
child not yet two years of age whose grandmother
asked and obtained for it *ut fidelis de sæculo recederet*
that it might die a Christian. But all candidates for
baptism, as about to be born again to Christ, were
spoken of as children and infants. Thus St. Augustine,
speaking of the great orator Victorinus says, *senex non
erubuit esse puer Christi et infans fontis Dei*—" Old as
he was, he was not ashamed to be the child of Christ,
and an infant at the font of God ". They were spoken
of in these terms for eight days after they had received
baptism, and during this period they continued to wear
the white garments, symbolic of innocence, which had
been put upon them as they came from the font.
The laying aside of these white garments on the octave
of Easter gave rise to the name by which we still know
the day, *Dominica in albis.* Here again we find proof
of the custom from the monuments, for we have not

[1] Duchesne, " Origines du Culte Chrétien ".

only an inscription in the cemetery of St. Callixtus which speaks of the baptismal robe which was buried with a woman who died within the octave of her baptism, but another of the year 463,[1] which records the same thing.

[1] De Rossi, " Roma Sott.," iii. p. 406.

CHAPTER IV.

The Witness of the Monuments to the Doctrine of the Holy Eucharist.

WE are by no means without testimonies of the doctrine of the Holy Eucharist, drawn from the writings of the Fathers and from other Christian documents. They are not always absolutely clear, especially in the earliest years, and this was often due to the *Disciplina arcani*, the rule which forbad any explicit mention of these Holy Mysteries in any writing which could get into heathen hands.

The most ancient of these testimonies is to be found in the "Didache," a document of the second century at latest, long lost, but recovered in 1883 in a manuscript of the eleventh century at Constantinople. Perhaps because of the discipline of which we have spoken it says nothing of the consecration, though it mentions the breaking of the bread. The Eucharistic prayers are to be recited after the Agape, or common meal. This is a proof of its great antiquity, for already by the beginning of the second century the change had been made which placed the Agape after instead of before the Eucharistic celebration.

A far more detailed description of the Eucharist is given to us in the "Apology" of St. Justin Martyr. It was written in a moment of comparative freedom from persecution, and so the discipline of secrecy was for the time a little relaxed. He speaks of lections from the Scriptures, of a homily or sermon, of the prayer of consecration and of the Communion. In another place he mentions the kiss of peace, which, he says, immediately preceded the actual reception by the faithful.

These passages, with the exception of a long liturgical prayer in the Epistle of St. Clement of Rome, and of a number of scattered allusions in the writings of St. Cyprian and other fathers, are almost the only ones during the age of persecution which have come down to us. The earliest actual liturgies do not go so far back. The writings of the Fathers after the peace of the Church have, possibly, to do with a more developed worship. The witness, therefore, of the monuments is thus of exceptional interest and importance as furnishing irrefragable proof that the belief of the faithful, in the days when active persecution made it impossible for them to set down their belief in clear terms in writing, was identical with that which is taught us by the works of the great Fathers of the Church at a later period.

Pictures in the Catacombs.

According to De Rossi the most ancient of the pictures of the catacombs which are concerned with the Holy Eucharist is that of the Crypts of Lucina. Here we have two paintings very much resembling one another, and placed symmetrically. In each is depicted a fish on a green background, carrying on his back, or as Mgr. Wilpert thinks, placed side by side with, a basket which contains bread, and in addition to the bread glasses filled with red wine. The allusion is, no doubt, to the miracles of the loaves and fishes, but the introduction of the wine emphasizes and renders necessary the Eucharistic application. The doctrine of Transubstantiation could scarcely be more vividly set forth. In the bread and wine we have the matter of the Sacrament ; in the fish which accompanies it the inner reality which the bread and wine become after consecration ; the true *Ichthus*, our Lord Jesus Christ. It would almost seem that St. Jerome must have had this very painting in his mind, as of course may very well have been the case, when he writes to Rusticus that "nothing can be richer than one who carries the Body of Christ in a basket made of twigs, and the Blood of Christ in a chalice of glass " ("ad Rusticum," Ep. 125 ; Migne, "P.L.," xxii. 1085). So again the Holy Eucharist is called by St. Paulinus "true bread and fish from living water" (Ep. xiii. ; "P.L.," lxi. 213).

Next in importance we must rank the famous painting in the Greek Chapel at Sta Priscilla, which is known as the *Fractio Panis*, and was discovered comparatively recently by Mgr. Wilpert in 1896. No one, certainly, has a better right than its discoverer to explain to us the meaning of this remarkable picture, which takes us back to the beginning of the second century and the age of St. Justin. It represents the actual liturgical action of the breaking of the bread. The priest is on the extreme left of the picture, and stretches out his hand to the bread which is before him. In front of him also stands the cup— two-handled and massive. Six persons are seated with him at the table, one of whom is a woman. Bread and fish are on the table ; five loaves and two fishes. On each side stand large baskets of bread.

Evidently we have here also an allusion to the miracles of our Lord. The number of the loaves and fishes, with the baskets on either side, make that abundantly clear. But the representation of a banquet and the chalice of wine make it no less clear that we have also a representation of the Holy Eucharist. It is, indeed, an actual picture of the offering of Holy Mass, as it was performed in the early second century, about the year 110. The guests have about them an air of real life, so the picture is not wholly mystical. In Mgr. Wilpert's opinion we have in it a real representation of an actual Mass celebrated in that chapel. Be that as it may, at least the doctrinal teaching of the symbolism is clear, and the lesson taught is the same as that of the fish we have just described—the transubstantiation of the bread and the wine into the Body and Blood of our Lord Jesus Christ.

There are several other similar representations of scarcely less importance. One, in the Chapel of the Sacraments at St. Callixtus, presents to us the tripod in the midst of the same baskets of bread. The tripod is thus a new Eucharistic symbol, and no doubt besides representing the Altar has reference to the Blessed Trinity. It appears with greater definiteness in another picture in the same Chapel of the Sacraments, where the tripod bears the loaf and the fish, and the priest extends his hands over it apparently in the very act of consecration. By his side is a female *Orante*, representing the Church in the attitude of worship. This picture forms only one of a series of three, each of which is of interest in this connection. The second is a banquet of seven disciples, of which we will speak immediately ; the third being a representation of the sacrifice of Abraham and Isaac. These two together give us the double aspect of the Eucharist, as communion and as sacrifice, each of which results from the consecration which is represented in the first picture.

The banquet of the seven disciples which forms the second picture of this group is only the earliest in-

9

stance of a subject of frequent occurrence.   Always the
number of the disciples is seven, never more nor less ;
and always bread and fish form the meal that is set
before them.   The scene is clearly that recorded in
Jn. xxi. 9, and represents the meal eaten by our
Lord after His Resurrection, at the Sea of Tiberias.
There are no baskets to suggest the miraculous
multiplication of the loaves and fishes, and the diners
are represented nude, as being fishermen.   Once again
the Fathers explain the picture, and tell us that the
fish roasted on the ashes is Christ Himself.   *Piscis
assus; Christus passus* (Aug., "Tract.," cxxiii. in Joan. ;
" P.L.," xxxv. 1966).

But this painting is only one type, though an
early one, of a great number of similar representations of Eucharistic banquets which we find in the
frescoes of this period.   Sometimes there are more
than seven feasters, and then the allusion is primarily
to the heavenly banquet, and only secondarily to the
Eucharist.   The fish in these pictures is rarely represented.   Sometimes the banquet is of the five wise
Virgins, carrying lighted torches, and here the application is the same.   There is, however, one very interesting fresco of the second century in the Catacomb
of Sta Domitilla, which we ought not to pass by.   It
represents, as may be seen in spite of the bad state of
the fresco, two persons seated at a tripod table on
which is bread and fish.   A server waits behind, which
is the peculiarity which distinguishes this picture from
many others.   It is developed in others of the third
century, especially at SS. Pietro e Marcellino.   Here
we have two women always as assistants.   The
inscriptions above them tell us who they are.   They
are Peace and Charity, who ought always to be
present at the Eucharistic feast.   The legend tells us
their office : IRENE DA CALDA, AGAPE MISCE MI,

The word *Misce* reminds us of the fact, which we should hardly otherwise have learned from these pictures, that water was always mixed with the wine at the Holy Eucharist, because of the belief that this had been done by our Blessed Lord at the Last Supper.

Another Eucharistic symbol which we must not omit to notice is the pail of milk. We find it in the representations of the Good Shepherd, sometimes on the back of a sheep, sometimes suspended from the pastoral staff, and sometimes simply by the side of the principal figure. In one representation at SS. Pietro e Marcellino, repeated in each corner of a vault, is the lamb carrying the vessel, but it is the vessel and not the lamb which bears the nimbus.[1] This alone would make it certain, were there any doubt in the matter, that here again we have a reference to the Holy Eucharist. We may compare the Acts of St. Perpetua, which are of the third century. She had a vision of the Good Shepherd, who appeared to her in prison. He gave her curdled milk to eat, and she received it as she had been accustomed to receive the Eucharist, with crossed hands and answering, Amen, after reception (Ruinart, " Acta Sincera "). So also St. Clement of Alexandria uses the same image when he says that " the Church nourishes her children with milk, and this milk . . . is the Body of Christ " (" Paedag.," i. vii.).

The grape, which is not rare on sepulchral monuments, has the same signification. We see it especially in the mosaics at Sta Costanze. The manna, which seems so obvious a symbol, especially in view of the sixth chapter of St. John, is very rare indeed. We see it, however, in one of the arcosolia at Sta Cyriaca.

There remains one more representation of frequent

[1] See *supra*, p. 86.

occurrence which has a Eucharistic application. It is
that of the Miracle of Cana.   St. Cyril of Jerusalem
asks why, "since the Lord at Cana changed water into
wine, which is akin to blood," it should be thought
"incredible that He should have turned bread into
His Body (" Cat.," xxii. 2).   Two frescoes of this subject survive at SS. Pietro e Marcellino, and have only
recently been brought to our knowledge.   In the first,
which dates from the first half of the third century, we
have the usual seven persons, four men and three
women, seated round a tripod table.   The ground is
strewn with green leaves.   A servant bearing a veiled
dish advances from the left towards the principal
guest.   In the foreground Christ touches with a wand
one of six great jars which are before him.   There is
no attempt at historical representation, and the miracle
is clearly used as a symbol of the Eucharist.   This is
made yet more certain by the symbols of baptism—
Moses and the rock and an actual baptism—which
are on either side.   The two great sacraments were
seldom divided in the thought of the time.

The other picture is a century later, and the application is clearer.   Seven persons again, all apparently men, are seated at a table with the usual tripod
bearing the fish in front.   A servant comes forward
bearing a glass filled with wine.   The companion
picture represents the multiplication of the bread.

All the instances we have hitherto given are from
Rome, but one other exists in the Catacombs at
Alexandria,[1] which was discovered in 1864.   The
picture is immediately behind the place where the
altar once stood.   It is divided into three portions by
trees.   In the centre is Christ bearing the nimbus and
seated on a throne.   He blesses loaves and fishes
presented by Peter and Andrew, and at his feet are

[1] Lowrie, " Monuments of the Early Church," 1901.

PORTION OF THE INSCRIPTION OF PECTORIUS AT AUTUN

From Cabrol's " Dictionnaire d'Archéologie Chrétienne " (Paris : Letouzey et Ané)

twelve baskets of bread. On each side were scenes of banquet. That on the left, much destroyed, was apparently a Eucharistic feast, for we still can read the words, "Those partaking of the eulogia of Christ". On the right, in like manner, fragments of inscriptions prove that the Marriage at Cana was represented. The application of the whole is obvious enough.

Inscriptions Concerning the Holy Eucharist.

To the general witness of the pictures of the catacombs we must add also the witness of the inscriptions. There are two most notable monuments, both of them of the second century, and both discovered far from Rome itself, which beyond all others claim a careful investigation at our hands. These are the famous *Stele* of Abercius, an account of the discovery of which has been already given in our last chapter, and a somewhat similar inscription, of a date not very much later, which was found at Autun in France in 1839. Both are in Greek, and it will be best for our present purpose to consider them together, as they mutually throw light upon one another. To take first the *Stele* of Abercius. This is the portion which has reference to the Holy Eucharist :—

"Faith everywhere led the way, and set before me for food the fish from the fountain, mighty and stainless (whom a pure virgin grasped), and gave this to friends to eat always, having good wine and giving the mixed cup with bread."

Compare with this the words of the inscription of Pectorius at Autun :—

"Celestial offspring of the Divine Fish, fortify thy heart, since thou hast received in the midst of mortals the immortal source of Divine love. Friend, rejoice thy soul with the water that ever gushes forth from the wisdom that gives treasures. Receive this sweet sustenance as the honey of the Saviour of the saints, eat with delight, holding the Fish in thy hands."

It is only by the symbolism of the Catacombs, as we have already explained it, that we are enabled to understand what is the hidden meaning of these two most important inscriptions. Without that key they would seem, as they must have seemed to hundreds of the heathen who read them when they were first erected, utterly meaningless and futile.

But, once we are possessed of the key, the whole is open to us. We have the fountain gushing from the rock, the rock that is Christ; the Wisdom that gives treasures to such as seek them. From that water of baptism, which flows from the stricken side of Christ, we are drawn forth by the rod of the fishermen; little fishes, the offspring of the Divine Fish. And not merely are we fishes, as sharers in the nature of that Divine Fish, but we are also fed on fish; and faith it is that gives us fish to eat. We hold that Fish in our hands, for that, as we learn from St. Cyril of Jerusalem, was the way in which the faithful were wont in those ages to receive Holy Communion. "Make thy left hand," he says, "a throne for thy right, which is about to receive thy King" ("Catech." xxiii. 21). Faith gives this Fish to her friends always "having good wine and giving the mixed cup with bread," and it is only through Faith that we know these elements to be really the true Fish from the fountain; the Fish that was born of a pure Virgin; mighty and without spot. The food is sweet as honey, the honey of the Saviour of the saints; it is the immortal source of Divine love, received in the midst of mortals. All through our lives it is ever with us, on the mountains and the plains the Good Shepherd gives it to us, and we are refreshed by it as we pass onwards on our journey homewards.

It would be difficult indeed to find a more explicit and definite exposition of the doctrine of the Real Presence of Christ in the Holy Eucharist, and of the transubstantiation of the bread and wine to become His true Body and Blood, than we have here in these two epitaphs, when once we have been given the key to their interpretation. They are earlier than almost all the purely literary evidence that remains to us in the writings of the fathers. In them we are listening to the voice of the second and third centuries; when it was still impossible to speak clearly on such subjects because of persecution. Mystical they are, of course, but not obscure. Indeed they could scarcely speak more plainly. It is almost with a shock of surprise that we find the doctrine of the twentieth century, as it is held and taught in the Catholic Church to-day thus definitely set out, engraved on imperishable stone, before a hundred years had passed from the time of our Lord's Ascension.

These inscriptions of Abercius from Phrygia, and of Pectorius from ancient Gaul testify to the definiteness of the doctrine thus held in union in the second and third centuries by Christians very widely divided by race and locality. The inscriptions of St. Damasus at Rome two or three hundred years later have a very different character. These latter were official monuments, set up by authority in a city which was not yet Christian, but in which Christianity was already free. We have seen how in the earlier centuries, all the essentials of the Catholic belief are already set forth, although they are shrouded in mystical and symbolical language. Let us see how the Church spoke at the end of the fourth century, when she had nothing to fear from speaking plainly.

Among the stories of the martyrs of the Valerian persecution there is none morebeautiful and more touching than that of the boy-martyr Tarcisius. He was an acolyte ; admitted, that is, to one of the lower orders of the clergy, and, no doubt, hoping in due time to be promoted to the priesthood. In this capacity he was entrusted with the Blessed Sacrament in order that he might carry it to some place where Christian prisoners were confined and so enable them to receive Holy Communion. Perhaps it was thought a boy would pass unchallenged where a priest would infallibly have been stopped and taken prisoner. He was not, however, so fortunate as to pass unnoticed, and was challenged by the pagans to say what it was that he was carrying. He would not answer them, nor, being unwilling to expose the Blessed Sacrament to insult, would he show them what he had in his possession. They set upon him with clubs and stones and so ill-treated him that he died under their blows, but when they came to search his hands and his garments, they could discover no sign of anything at all. The Blessed Sacrament had disappeared. His body was buried by the Christians in the Catacomb of St. Callixtus, and now rests in the Church of San Silvestro in Capite. Over his shrine St. Damasus put up the following inscription :—

TARCISIVM SANCTVM CHRISTI SACRAMENTA
  FERENTEM
CVM MALESANA MANVS PETERET VULGARE
  PROFANIS
IPSE ANIMAM POTIVS VOLVIT DIMITTERE CÆSVS
PRODERE QVAM CANIBVS RABIDIS CÆLESTIA
  MEMBRA

When the evil band sought to profane the sacraments of Christ, borne by holy Tarcisius, he preferred to lose his life under their blows, than to betray the heavenly limbs to those maddened dogs.

What in the second century could only be spoken of

under a symbol, in the fourth could be said plainly. The bread and the wine, say the earlier inscriptions, are not what they seem, they are the *Ichthus*—the Divine Fish—Jesus Christ, the Son of God, the Saviour. St. Damasus teaches precisely the same doctrine, but he teaches it in plainer language. The bread and the wine, as they were to outward seeming, which Tarcisius was carrying to the Christian prisoners, were other than they seemed to be. Had the pagan mob obtained their wish and succeeded in wresting them from the martyr as he fell, it would not have been mere bread and wine, but *cœlestia membra*, the heavenly limbs of our Lord and Saviour that they would have outraged. The symbolism of the second century receives its full interpretation in the explicit words of the late inscription.

So through the ages the voice of the monuments sounds forth, bearing witness to the fact that what the Church teaches and believes now, when a score of centuries have passed over her head, that also she believed and taught in the fourth century, in the first days of the peace of the Church, and that also she held with no less clearness and certainty while the storms of persecution were still beating around her. We could hardly ask for a proof more striking and unanswerable of the marvellous and unchanging unity of Catholic doctrine in all ages.

CHAPTER V.

The Witness of the Monuments as to Other Rites and Ceremonies of the Church.

THE pre-eminence of the two great Sacraments, Baptism and the Holy Eucharist, is exceedingly clear in the catacombs, and there are not many pictures or inscriptions which deal with the other sacraments and ceremonies of the Church. It may, however, be worth while to bring together a few scattered testimonies which throw light upon the doctrine, or elucidate the ritual which was practised in those earliest centuries.

Confirmation.

Although, of course, Confirmation is a Sacrament altogether distinct from Baptism, and in no way necessarily connected with it, it was the custom of the early Church, in the case of children no less than of adults, to administer it always in the same function and immediately after baptism had been received. Before the time of Tertullian no one of the Fathers makes any explicit mention of Confirmation as distinct from Baptism, no doubt because of this custom of conferring both together, but from the middle of the second century onwards the distinction is clear. Confirmation is spoken of sometimes as "imposition of hands," sometimes as "chrism," or as "sealing". The actual word "confirmation" appears first at the Council of Elvira (Can. xxxviii.), where it is enacted that any who have been baptized by laics must be brought as soon as possible to the Bishop that he may confirm them (*perficere possit*) by imposition of hands. So also St. Leo ("ad Nicet." vii.) says that those who have been baptized by heretics must be confirmed by the invocation of the Holy Ghost and by laying on of hands. When it became usual for priests to baptize, and this office was no longer normally confined to bishops, an extension of the same reasoning brought about our present practice concerning this Sacrament.

After the candidate had come up from the font having received Holy Baptism, he was conducted to the Bishop, who was seated solemnly upon his throne. For this reason the place of the *cathedra*, or Bishop's throne, in early times was always close to the Baptistery. There is a chair of this kind, cut out of the rock in the *Cœmeterium Ostrianum*, close to the place where baptism was administered. So again it was in the Baptistery at St. Peter's that St. Damasus placed the Chair of Peter, and he connected it with the ceremonies there enacted by the following inscription :—

VNA PETRI SEDES VNVM VERVMQVE LAVACRVM

One is the Chair of Peter, one also and true is baptism.

St. Ennodius of Pavia speaks of this chair in terms which make the connection even more clear. "The neophytes," he says, "go from the dripping threshold to the gestatorial chair of the Apostolic confession ; amid abundant tears called forth by joy the gifts of grace are doubled" ("Libellus pro Synodo," *ad fin.*).

Another inscription of St. Damasus in the same Vatican Baptistery makes a yet clearer allusion to Confirmation, for it speaks not only of the "signing" of the candidates by the Bishop, but also of the "cross" received by them through that signing :—

ISTIC INSONTES COELESTI FLVMINE LOTAS
  PASTORIS SVMMI DEXTERA SIGNAT OVES
HVC VNDIS GENERATE VENI QVO SANCTVS AD VNVM
  SPIRITVS VT CAPIAS TE SVA DONA VOCAT
TV CRVCE SVSCEPTA MVNDI VITARE PROCELLAS
  DISCE MAGIS MONITOS HAC RATIONE LOCI [1]

Here and there we meet with epitaphs which record the fact of Confirmation, but they are naturally rare. Fabretti, however, has preserved one which told how two persons, a husband and wife, named Catervius and Severina, died immediately after receiving Baptism and Confirmation from a Bishop named Probianus.

QVOS DEI SACERDVS PROBIANVS LAVIT ET
VNXIT. [2]

Whom Probianus, the priest of God, washed and anointed.

Here is another which comes from Rome :—

PICENTIAE LEGITIMAE
NEOPHYTAE DIE V KAL. SEP.
CONSIGNATAE A LIBERIO PAPA. [3]

To Picentia, a true neophyte, who was confirmed by Pope Liberius.

Marriage.

The Christian view of marriage in the second century is set forth by Tertullian. "Whence," he asks, "shall I be able to tell the happiness of the marriage

[1] " Inscr. Christ.," ii. p. 139.
[2] Fabretti, " Corp. Inscr. Ital.," x. 505.
[3] Oderico, " Syll. vet. inscr.," p. 268.

which the Church arranges (*conciliat*), the sacrifice
confirms and the blessing seals." [1] The phrase is
short enough, but it puts us in possession of the facts
that in the second century Christian marriage was not
merely a civil function, but was already regarded as a
sacrament, to be entered upon before the Church, to
be united to the offering of the Holy Sacrifice and the
reception of Holy Communion, and finally to be sealed
by the benediction of the priest.

A sarcophagus was discovered in the Villa Albani
some years ago which gives a representation of a
Christian marriage, a subject which is very rarely met
with in such monuments. The sculpture is a good
deal damaged, and only the right-hand portion now
remains intact. On the right is a male figure wearing
the tunic and pallium, holding in his left hand a
volume, while with his right he grasps the hand of
another figure, which has now disappeared through the
decay of the marble. In the middle, between the two
figures, and beneath the two hands then joined, is an
open book, placed upon a small lectern. Above, between the two, there appears among the clouds the
bust of the Saviour, who with outstretched arms holds
two crowns which He is in the act of placing upon the
heads of the two figures. [2]

The monument appears to be of the fourth century
and is, therefore, the earliest representation of the
Sacrament of Matrimony which has survived. If the
female figure were still visible we should, doubtless,
find it veiled, for this custom, already in use among
the pagans, was preserved by the Christians. The
open book is clearly that of the Gospel, on which the
promise of mutual fidelity was made. The crown was
a regular part of the ceremony of marriage among the

---

[1] " Ad uxorem," ii. 9.
[2] Marucchi, " Studi in Italia," 1882.

heathen,[1] and was at first refused by Christians [2] as unlawful, but adopted at a later time from the East, where, indeed, it seems never to have been entirely disused. The crowns were placed on the heads of the newly married pair, immediately after the benediction, and were worn not only till the end of the ceremony but for eight days afterwards, when the couple came once more to the church in order to have the crowns solemnly removed. The ceremony had always more prominence in the East than in the West, and the prayers which accompanied the action may be found in the "Euchologion".[3]

The ring as a symbol of matrimonial union was already introduced, but hardly enjoyed the prominence which it has at present. It is mentioned by Tertullian, who speaks of it as the only gold a respectable woman ought to wear.[4] Several of such rings have come down to us bearing inscriptions. Here is one of the fourth century :—

VENANTI VIVAS IN DEO CVN SERCHA.
Venantius, live in God with Sercha.

Many others could be given.

Under Pope Callixtus, A.D. 218, the Church took a very important step. The law of the land declared the marriage between a woman of the highest rank, *clarissima*, and a man of servile condition or a freedman to be *ipso facto* null and void. The Church declared such unions to be in her eyes valid. De Rossi believes that he has discovered in an inscription at the cemetery of Domitilla a commemoration of such a marriage,

---

[1] Cf. Eurip., "Iphigenia in Aulide,," 905.
[2] Cf. Justin M., "Apol.," ix. ; Tertull., "Apol.," i. 42 ; Clem. Alex., " Pædag.," ii. 8.
[3] Goar, " Euchol.," pp. 396, 400.
[4] " Apol.," 6.

valid in the eyes of the Church though null in that of the State.[1]

The ordinary phrase by which those united in Christian marriage were wont to describe themselves was as *Conservi*, Fellow-servants, with or without the addition of the words Christi or Dei. Thus when St. Jerome writes to Paulinus about his wife Terasia, he calls her *Sanctam conservam tuam tecum in Domino militantem* [2]—Thy holy fellow-servant who fights at thy side in the Lord. So in many a monument of the period we find the term used :—

PLOTIVS TERTIVS ET FAVSTINA CONSERVI DEI FECERVNT SIBI IN PACE. X.

Plotius Tertius and Faustina, fellow-servants of God, made this for themselves. In the peace of Christ.

Sometimes the same phrase is found in Greek. One was found in Catania in which the wife styles herself :—[3]

ϹΥΝΔΟΥΛΗ ΕΝ ΧΡΙϹΤΩ

A fellow-servant in Christ.

Penance.

M. De Rossi held that the representation of the paralytic, healed and carrying his bed, which we meet with in the Chapel of the Sacraments at the cemetery of St. Callixtus, was intended to convey the idea of penance, just as other pictures in the same series undoubtedly did represent the Sacraments of Baptism and the Holy Eucharist. But this is now generally admitted not to be so. The paralytic represented is not, probably, the paralytic of Capharnaum (Mt. ix. 2), which would make the application obvious, but rather the paralytic of the pool of Bethesda, and this would naturally suggest rather baptism than penance. The

---

[1] " Bull. d' arch. crist.," 1880, p. 65.   [2] " Ep.," 58.
[3] Torremuzza, " Inscr. Sic.," p. 260, 15.

subject of penance in the catacombs is in any case rare, but there is no doubt a reference to it in the most frequent of all the representations, that of the Good Shepherd bearing on His shoulders the sheep that was lost. Of course the reference here again is not exclusive. Christians when they looked upon this symbol were reminded also of the constant care which Christ had for His Church in this world, and especially of His care for each individual soul in the moment of death, and in the life that lies beyond the grave. But neither of these applications exhaust the significance or even give so full a meaning as does that of penance ; so that we are justified in considering this to be the primary and most important interpretation of the symbol.

It would not be possible here to go into the details of the system of public penance, as evolved and carried out in the Church of the first centuries. In any case death brought an end of such penance, and so it is seldom noted on the tomb. The only instances which have come down to us are from Gaul.

Here is one from Aix les Bains, with a consular date :—

> HIC IN PACE QVIESCIT ADIVTOR QVI POST
> ACCEPTAM POENITENTIAM
> MIGRAVIT IN DOMINVM.

Another from Lyons, also with a consular date :—

> IN HOC TVMVLO REQVIESCET BONAE MEMORIAE
> RELIGIOSA QVI EGIT POENITENTIAM ANNOS
> VIGINTI ET DVOS ET VIXE IN PACE ANNVS
> SEXAGINTA QVINQVE.

Funeral Rites and Ceremonies.

As far as was possible the Church reduced the ceremonies of burial which were customary among the heathen, inasmuch as many of them were of a character which it was impossible to reconcile with her own teaching, or to free from superstitious meanings. At the same time very much was continued and adapted, though very often with a different interpretation. Any one who desires to make an exhaustive study of the ceremonies of burial as they existed in the early Church, will do well, in the first place, to familiarize himself with the customs of the heathen world at Rome at the same period, and also with those of the Jews. He will find that much of the Christian ceremonial had its roots far back in times that were long before the coming of Christianity.

So soon as the body was cold, and it was quite certain that death had taken place, the corpse was carefully washed, and then was laid in linen clothes with spices and unguents. The whole process recalls the accounts of our Lord's burial at Jerusalem, and no doubt this was constantly present to their minds. It was carried out to burial with a good deal of ceremony, even in times of active persecution, processions being formed with lights and torches, and clergy following on the way. These acts of reverence to the dead were not hindered by the Romans, except during a very few periods, and the catacombs themselves, as we have seen, were protected by the common law, and therefore safe from profanation.

The most important matter connected with the burial of the dead was, of course, the offering of the Holy Sacrifice. This was done before the body was buried, when it was brought to the church. This Mass was called the Mass *dormitionis* or *depositionis*. When this was finished there came the prayers at the sepulchre, and afterwards, on the third, the seventh, and the thirtieth days, there were additional solemn offerings of the Holy Mass for the soul of the deceased, that he might obtain a merciful judgment. These Masses for the dead took place, in the days of persecution, close to the actual grave in the catacombs. This was the object of the many little chambers which have been excavated there. Such little chapels have not to do with the *cultus* of the martyrs, but rather with masses for the souls of those who were buried in the vicinity. In some cases seats are provided, cut in the rock. The object of these was to accommodate the relations and others who assembled there not only to hear Mass, but also, in conjunction with the clergy, to recite psalms and hymns for the soul of the departed. We have thus, already developed in the catacombs, the beginnings of the whole system of prayer for the dead which has continued in the Church ever since.

A word ought to be said, before we leave the subject, upon one of the most difficult and obscure of all archæological and liturgical questions; the connection, namely, between the ancient Agape and the funerals of the dead.

The ancients celebrated in the honour of the dead certain funeral repasts, which were in their eyes of the nature of an offering. Such a celebration was considered altogether a necessary part of funeral obsequies, without it the soul would lack something in the other world. The funeral feast was not, primarily, for the refreshment of the living, it was an offering for the repose and happiness of the dead. To suppose that it was merely commemorative would be altogether a mistake. The wine and the milk were poured out upon the tomb, nor in the earliest times did any living person partake of the food that was brought. It was for the dead, and for the dead alone. Only in later times did the living share in it at all; nor, even then, was the other side lost sight of. In the first and second centuries, although this pagan ceremony had become a meal eaten by the relations at or near the tomb, the aspect of an offering for the dead had by no means passed out of sight.

Under the system of *collegia*, or burial guilds, which we have described in an earlier chapter, the funeral feast was a recognized part of the expenditure for each member. The survivors met together on certain regular occasions, and ate a meal in common at their place of meeting, which was commonly annexed to, or at least in close proximity to, the spot where they were buried.

Christians apparently acted outwardly in the same way as their heathen contemporaries. They, too, met at the catacombs for their funeral celebrations. As with the heathen, so also with them, the proceedings had a double aspect—a feast for the living and an offering for the dead. The offering for the dead, however, was in their case no mere pouring out of wine and milk upon the grave; no mere sacrifice of an animal to procure the repose of the dead; but was the offering, under the form of bread and wine of the one, true, pure, and eternal sacrifice for the remission of sins. And just as our Blessed Lord in instituting the Holy Eucharist had chosen to do so at a solemn and religious meal, so also did His followers after Him connect the Holy Mass with a similar meal taken in common, which was called the Agape. All Christians there met together, whatever their degree and rank, and all shared in the repast. We know very little about the details of these meetings, all is shrouded almost in absolute obscurity. But it seems likely that, although the Agape soon led to abuses, and, consequently, was separated from the actual offering of the Holy Eucharist at a comparatively early date, it was yet kept in being in connection with funerals by the obvious advantage it presented. It enabled Christians to conform outwardly, even in detail, with the law and practice which regulated the *collegia*, and was, therefore, of a very real and practical utility which ensured its continuance long after it would otherwise have passed into oblivion.

We have in the Catacombs of Domitilla, in the well-known fresco of the *Fractio panis* in the *Cappella Greca*, a representation which brings home to us precisely this double aspect of the celebrations of the catacombs. On the other hand, it is the Holy Eucharist; the symbols of the baskets and of the fishes prove that no less than the action of the principal figure; but, on the other hand, it still has very much the appearance of an ordinary meal in which the worshippers are engaged.

But the whole subject is too full of difficulty and too obscure to allow us to speak upon it with any kind of certainty.[1] It is, however, too important to be altogether ignored in any study of the funeral customs of early Christianity.

[1] For an examination of the whole subject, see the study by Père Leclercq in the " Dict. d'arch. chrétienne," s.v. " Agape ".

BAPTISM OF CHRIST AND EUCHARISTIC FEAST

From a sarcophagus in the Lateran Museum

From Marucchi's "I Monumenti del Museo Cristiano Pio-Lateranense" (Milan : Ulrico Hoepli)

CHAPTER VI.

The Witness of the Monuments to the Communion of Saints.

As we wander through the halls of the Museum of Christian Antiquities, which now occupies the ancient Palace of the Lateran, and see the walls covered with inscriptions which have been brought thither from the various catacombs by which Rome is surrounded, or, still more, if we obtain the services of a guide and descend ourselves to those long and dreary passages excavated by the earliest Christians in the tufa rock, we can hardly fail to be struck with the wealth of evidence around us. These stones were never meant to play their parts in any controversy of doctrine; they were not intended to be brought into any kind of prominence, or even to be read by any eyes other than those of the immediate friends and acquaintances of the deceased person who is commemorated, and precisely for this reason they afford the most vivid and satisfying evidence that is possible to imagine as to the beliefs and practice in those early ages on the subject of the Communion of Saints. These men who cut these touching epitaphs on the stones that closed in the mortal remains of their dear ones, were not men who sorrowed without hope. They knew that those whom they thus laid to rest *in peace*—the word itself has additional pathos when we realize the state of persecution and fear in which the survivors were still living—were not lost to them, but had only gone before to that place of rest where all in turn hoped to be permitted to follow them. They made no picture of a state of mere sleep and unconsciousness, uninterrupted until the day of judgment, such as some later Christians have taught is the fate of those who die in the Lord, but thought of their dead as living more truly than before, and praying for those whom they had left behind, but still held in loving remembrance.

Prayer for the Dead.

We should hardly expect to find in a cemetery such as are the catacombs any clear statement of belief in the pains of purgatory. There can be no doubt as to the belief of modern Catholics on that subject, and yet a visit to a Catholic cemetery of the present time, and a study of the epitaphs inscribed on the graves will hardly supply us even with an allusion to the subject. The thoughts of the living with regard to the dead express themselves in two ways. They realize that the dead have need of their prayers, and so they arrange for Masses to be said and prayers to be offered on their behalf. But they remember also that although for a time suffering may be needed by the souls of the dead in order that they may thus attain to greater happiness, yet those souls are already "in peace," that the trial is over and the goal attained, and that, therefore, words of joy and of hope are most appropriate upon their last resting-places.

Bearing this in mind and remembering always that we should apply to these memorials of the dead just the same canons of interpretation that we should to similar inscriptions in a modern graveyard, we go on to examine what the catacombs have to teach us.

We find, first, a formula which, especially in the later graves, has become almost universal. It is the formula IN PACE, which meets us everywhere, so that it is no exaggeration to say that we can appeal to instances which can be counted by the thousand. Like the corresponding formula which has taken its place in more modern times, the three letters R.I.P., it is essentially a prayer, although the actual petition is not formally expressed. It is an aspiration, an ex-

EPITAPH OF A BOY.

(*From Marucchi's "I Monumenti del Museo Cristiano Pio-Lateran ense"* (Hoepli, Milan).)

pression of desire that it may be so with the departed soul, as well as an expression of conviction that this really is the case. The words are really of Jewish origin, and have been taken over from the Jews by Christians to express the condition of those who die in Christ. Here are a few examples, from the earliest cemeteries :—

ΦΙΛΟΥΜΕΝΗ ΕΝ ΕΙΡΕΝΗ COY ΤΟ ΠΝΕΥΜΑ

Philumena, may thy soul be in peace.

MAXIMIANVS SATVRNINA DORMIT IN PACA

Maximianus Saturnina, sleeps in peace.

BENEMERENTI IN PACE LIBERA QVE BIXIT A. XI.

NEOFITA.

To Libera well-deserving in peace, who lived 11 *years.*
A Neophyte.

ΦΟΡΤΟΥΝΑΤΟΥϹ ΕΥΜΕΝ . . . ΚΟΙΟΤΕΙ ΙΝ ΡΑΚΕ
Fortunatus Eumenes lies here in peace.

ARCESSITVS AB ANGELIS QVI VIXIT
ANN. XXII.   MESIS VIII.   DIEB. VIII.   IN PACE.

Fetched by the angels, who lived 22 *years* 8 *months*
8 *days.   In peace.*

Very often the formula is abbreviated.   Thus we
meet sometimes with such forms as these: IN P.—IN
PC,—I P,—E I (*ἐν εἰρήνῃ*)—EN EIP.

The instances already quoted are for the most part
mere statements, into which the prayer, if it exists at
all, has to be read.   Here are some of a more definite
kind :—

ΕΙΡΗΝΗ ϹΟΥ ΤΗ ΨΥΧΗ ΖΩϹΙΜΗ
Peace be to thy soul, Zosima,

ΕΙΡΗΝΗ ΤΕ ΦΟΡΤΥΝΑΤΕ ΘΥΓΑΤΡΙ ΓΛΥΚΤΑΤΗ
and peace be to Fortunata, my sweetest daughter.

HILARIS VIVAS CVM TVIS FELICITER SEMPER
REFRIGERIS IN PACE DEI

Hilaris, may you live for ever happy with your friends,
may you be refreshed in the peace of God.

The formula IN PACE, general as it is, is yet by no
means universal.   Sometimes the prayer is rather for
refreshment :—

BOLOSA DEVS TIBI REFRIGERET
Bolosa, may God refresh you.

REFRIGERA DEVS ANIMA
O God, refresh the soul of. . . .

The following narration, drawn from the authentic Acts of St. Perpetua, which date from the very beginning of the third century, may help us to understand the meaning which this word *refrigerium* conveyed to those who originally placed it on these tombs. Perpetua, when in prison waiting for her martyrdom, had

EPITAPH OF A VIRGIN NAMED BELUCIA.

(From Marucchi's " I Monumenti del Museo Cristiano Pio-Lateran ense " (Hoepli, Milan).)

a vision in which she saw her young brother, Dinocrates, who had died a short time before at the age of seven years from cancer in the face. She saw him coming out of a dark place, very pale, and disfigured by a terrible wound in his face. He was sad and depressed, and went wandering hither and thither like one who had suffered some great loss. She could not reach him to help him for there was a great gulf between them. There was a great fountain in the place where Dinocrates was, and it seemed that he was very thirsty, for he kept trying to drink from it, but could not because he was too small to be able to reach it. As she could help him in no other way she began to pray for him, and she continued doing so after this vision until the eve of her martyrdom. Then she had another vision. She saw the same place as before, but quite transformed, shining with light, and looking like a beautiful garden. In this garden was Dinocrates happy and cheerful, playing about in white clothes. The tip of the fountain was lower down and from it he drank continually and was refreshed (*et vidi Dinocratem refrigerantem*). Thus she understood that her prayers had reached him and helped him, and that now he was refreshed in the heavenly kingdom.[1]

HPAKΛIA PΩMH IC ANAPAYCIN COY H ΨYXH

Heraclea Roma, may thy soul go into rest.

The transliteration in this case is interesting. The Greek word εἰς appears as IC.

In a great many instances the prayer for the departed is for light :—

ETERNA LVX TIBI TIMOTHEA IN XP

Timothea, mayest thou have eternal light in Christ.

[1] Ruinart, " Acta sincera ".

NE QVANDO ADVMBRETVR SPIRITVS

May his spirit never be overshadowed,

and very frequently indeed is for life eternal :—

A.   EPENEA VIVAS IN DEO   Ω

Irenaea, mayest thou live in God.

AGAPE . VIBES . IN . AETERNVM

Agapus, mayest thou live for ever.

ΕΝ ΘΕΩ ΜΕΤΑ ΠΑΝΤΩΝ ΠΟΝΤΙΑΝΕ ΖΗCΗC

Mayest thou live, O Pontianus, with all in God.

This last is of especial interest. It is not actually an epitaph, but a *graffito*, an inscription, that is, written on the wall by some visitor to the tomb. It is in the chapel known as the Papal Crypt at St. Callixtus, and was done while the plaster was still wet. We can, therefore, date it with absolute accuracy. It must have been written at the precise time when the relics of Pope Pontianus, having been brought back from Sardinia where he had died in exile, were buried in this very chapel by St. Fabian in 245.

Prayers of the Departed for the Living.

Hitherto the epitaphs we have been considering have been confined to prayers for those who lie buried in the tombs. It is clear from them that the belief of the early Church was definite in its teaching that the souls of the departed were benefited by prayers made on their behalf. Let us now pass on to consider what light is thrown by the inscriptions on the belief of those times concerning the value of the prayers of those who had passed away for the friends they had left behind.

It was not only for the prayers of the saints, properly so called, that the early Christians asked. We find everywhere engraved on the stones in the catacombs requests for the prayers of the dead, and there is no reason whatever to think that wherever this occurs we have the tomb of a martyr. It is evident that the belief of those centuries was that the holy souls could intercede effectively for those whom they had left behind, even before they had themselves attained to the Beatific Vision. Here are a few examples :—

IANVARIA BENE REFRIGERA
ET ROGA PRO NOS

Januaria, be thou well refreshed, and intercede for us.

ATTICE SPIRITVS TVVS
IN BONO ORA PRO PAREN
TIBVS TVIS

Atticus, thy spirit is in happiness, pray for thy parents.

The next one is imperfect, but sufficient remains for our purpose. It is in the cemetery of Domitilla :—

N
IBAS
IN PACE ET PETE
PRO NOBIS

Mayst thou live in peace and intercede for us.

PETE PRO PARENTIBVS TVIS
MATRONATA MATRONA
QVE VIXIT AN I D LII

Matronata Matrona, who lived one year and fifty-two days, pray for thy parents.

Here the prayers are asked of one who died in infancy before she can have known what prayers meant.

ATTICE DORMI IN PACE
DE TVA INCOLVMITATE
SECVRVS ET PRO NOSTRIS
PECCATIS PETE SOLLICITVS

Atticus, sleep in peace, secure of thy salvation, and pray
earnestly for our sins.

KARA MNHMONEYE MOY

Cara (or " dear one "), remember me.

GENTIANVS FIDELIS IN PACE
QVI VIXIT ANNIS XXI MENS VIII
DIES XVI ET IN ORATIONIS TVIS
ROGES PRO NOBIS QVIA SCIMVS
TE IN ℞

Gentian, a Christian, in peace.
Who lived xxi years viii months xvi days.
In thy prayers intercede for us, for we know
thou art in Christ.

SVTI PETE
PRO NOS
VT SALVI SIMVS

Sutius, pray for us, that we may be saved.

SABBATI DVLCIS
ANIMA PETE ET RO
GA PRO FRATRES ET
SODALES TVOS.

Sabbatius, sweet soul, intercede and make petition
for thy brothers and companions.

Invocation of Saints.

In the days of persecution the value to the Church
of the witness borne by the martyrs who laid down
their lives for the Faith was seen to be of paramount importance. It was to the martyrs, therefore, and practically to them alone, that the thoughts

of Christians turned when they needed an intercession with God. They alone were canonized in anything resembling our modern sense. The word *martyr* could only be placed on a tomb by the permission of the Bishop and after an inquiry duly held, and it was the formal permission to the faithful to pay religious honours at the tomb of one who had been thus qualified.

Most of the evidence, therefore, which is available on this subject comes to us, not so much from the formal epitaphs of those who had thus given their life for the faith as from a yet more interesting and living source of information. It is from the *graffiti*, the scribbled notes on the walls of the chapels in which the martyrs were buried, left by pilgrims who had come to seek their intercession, that we learn most of what Christians then felt and believed on this subject. Very many of these *graffiti* remain to this day, and Christian archæology has no branch which is of more vivid interest for its votaries.

At the cemetery of St. Basilla we read

DOMINA BASILLA COMMANDAMVS TIBI CRESCEN-
TINVS ET MICINA FILIA NOSTRA CRESCEN . . . QVE
VIXIT MEN X ET DIES . . .

O Lady Basilla, we, Crescentinus and Micina, commend to thee our daughter Crescentina who lived ten months and . . . days.

Another epitaph, too long to quote in full, appeals at the end to the martyrs to help the soul of the departed:—

MARTYRES SANCTI IN MENTE HA
VITE MARIA

Ye holy martyrs, keep Maria in your mind.

REFRIGERET TIBI DOMINVS IPPOLYTVS

May St. Hippolytus refresh thee.

Here is an ancient example from the cemetery

of St. Priscilla, which appeals to the intercession of
St. Peter :—

> RVTA OMNIBVS SVBDITA ET ADFA
> BILIS BIBET IN NOMINE PETRI
> IN PACE ☧

*May Ruta, who was humble and kind to all, live in the
name of Peter. In the peace of Christ.*

> PROCVLA CL FEMINA
> FAMVLA DEI
> A TERRA AD MARTYRES

*Procula, a woman of noble family, the servant of God.
From earth to the Martyrs.*

Here is a bold instance in which the martyrs are
joined to the name of God and of Christ :—

> NVTRICATVS DEO CHRISTO
> MARTYRIBVS

Nourished by God, Christ, and the Martyrs.

These are instances from ordinary tombs, but the
evidence of the *graffiti*, or inscriptions scratched on the
walls of the crypts in which the martyrs lie buried,
is of even greater interest and importance. Near the
papal crypt in the cemetery of St. Callixtus, the whole
wall is covered with writing. One after another the
pilgrims as they came to visit that sacred spot, so full
of sacred memories of the past, wrote down, as they
waited for the doors to open, the desires and aspirations
which had brought them thither. These *graffiti*, written
in bad Latin, generally wrongly spelt and scribbled one
on the top of another, presented a problem which might
have baffled any archæologist. However, the patience
of De Rossi was equal to the task, and the results of
his patient labours are truly marvellous. His words
have been often quoted, but are too valuable to be
omitted. "Here," writes a pilgrim, "is the true

Jerusalem, adorned with the martyrs of the Lord."
"Live in Christ," "Live in God," "Live in the
Eternal," "Rest in peace," wrote others, thinking
of the dear ones they had lost. Pope St. Xystus
seems to have been the object of special devotion.

GRAFFITI IN THE PAPAL CRYPT AT ST. CALLIXTUS.
(*From Marucchi's " Eléments d'Archæologie," Desclée De Brouwer et Cie.*)

He had been beheaded in the cemetery of Prætextatus,
on the other side of the Appian Way ; but his remains had been transferred to the papal crypt, where
his throne, dyed with his blood, was also to be seen.
"Remember us in thy prayers"—*In mente habeas in*

orationibus—is a formula used by many pilgrims who under it inscribed their names and those of their friends. " Pray for Marcian, my adopted child," asks one. Another requests the martyr to obtain for his father and his brothers eternal rest and union with the supreme good. A mother asks that Vereumdus and his family may have a happy journey. Many similar invocations are unfinished, or have become unreadable like so many prayers which human life cannot express, but which God hears in silence.[1]

Though fifteen centuries separate us from those times, we may still follow the track of one of the visitors in the galleries of the cemetery of St. Callixtus. He had apparently come to pray for a certain Sophronia, either his wife, his daughter, or his mother. Before entering the porch of the main sanctuary he wrote, *Sofronia . . . vibas cum tuis*—" Sophronia, mayest thou live with thine". A few paces farther on, at the door of another chapel, he repeats this formula with a slight addition: *Sofronia (vibas) in Domino*—" Sophronia, mayest thou live in the Lord ". Farther on, near the *arcosolium* of yet another chapel, he has written in large letters these words: *Sofronia dulcis, semper vives Deo*—" Sweet Sophronia, thou wilt always live in God"; and just below he has again scribbled, *Sofronia vives*—" Sophronia, thou shalt live ". It would seem as if this pilgrim, as he progressed further and further down this subterranean passage which was sanctified by the presence of the bodies of St. Xystus, St. Cecilia, St. Fabian, St. Pontian, and so many other martyrs less known to fame, experienced varying feelings. He had come full of anxiety for the salvation of one he loved, but little by little this feeling changed to hope, then to confidence, and finally to certainty, and he returned

[1] De Rossi, " Roma Sott.," ii. pp. 13-20 ; cf. also plates xxix-xxxiv.

from his pilgrimage convinced that his prayer had been granted.[1]

Veneration of the Martyrs.

When once the peace of the Church had come, and the tombs of the martyrs might safely be venerated, then indeed was no lack of honour done to them. In order that churches might be built where their bodies rested, and in order that their tombs might serve as the high altars of those churches, hundreds and even thousands of graves must have been destroyed. At Sta Agnese the long flight of steps which leads down into the church speaks eloquently, even now, of this destruction. There was no thought of moving the body of the saint to a church above ground, the church must come to the martyr, where she lay deep down in the catacombs under the ground. Here in churches like this the anniversaries of the martyrs were kept with the utmost splendour. But those to whom no churches were built were not neglected. To their graves the crowds of pilgrims went, from every nation on the earth, and for their guidance from one sacred tomb to another "Itineraries" were compiled, which in these later days have been the principal aid by which the various cemeteries have been identified.

To Romans themselves no greater honour was obtainable in the fourth and fifth centuries, than to be buried, not in the cemeteries above ground which were now everywhere being provided, but down below in the catacombs, and, if possible, close to the remains of some one of the martyrs. Numbers of paintings, of the highest interest and value, have been destroyed by later graves, which have thus intruded. Here, again, many epitaphs record the desire and its accom-

[1] De Rossi, "Roma Sott.," i, 259 ; ii, 15 ; cf, plate xxxi, 2, 4. 7.

plishment. We must content ourselves with quoting only one or two :—

SERPENTIVS EMIT LOCVM
A QVINTO FOSSORE
AD SANCTVM CORNELIVM

Serpentius bought himself a grave from Quintus the fossor, close to St. Cornelius.

IN CRYPTA NOBA RETRO SANCTOS
In a new crypt behind the saints.

Here, since there was no longer room in the original crypt in which the saints lay buried, a new gallery had been excavated to enable those who desired it to be buried in close contiguity with the martyrs, though in another gallery.

We can see how widespread the desire was from the writings of the Fathers. St. Gregory Nazianzus, St. Ambrose, and St. Paulinus of Nola, all had their relatives buried near the martyrs. The practice grew to an abuse, and the inscription on the grave of Sabinus, Archdeacon of Rome in the fifth century, rebukes those who desired to be buried there, saying :—

NIL IVVAT IMO GRAVAT TVMVLIS HAERERE PIORVM
SANCTORVM MERITIS OPTIMA VITA PROPE EST

It is useless and even dangerous to lie close to the tombs of the saints ; a good life brings one nearer to the merits of the saints.

In the same spirit St. Damasus, when he put up his inscription in the crypt of the martyrs, records his desire to be buried there himself, and the way in which he had resisted the temptation :—

HIC FATEOR DAMASVS VOLVI MEA CONDERE
MEMBRA
SED CINERES TIMVI SANCTOS VEXARE PIORVM

Here I, Damasus, confess that I wished to hide my limbs, but I feared to disturb the holy ashes of the saints.

Burial in the catacombs went on until the invasion of the Goths in 408. At that time these cemeteries, lying outside the walls, were largely pillaged by these invaders in search of treasure. After the invasions were over it was felt that the relics of the martyrs ought no longer to be left exposed to such dangers, and the process of translation to safer spots within the city, which would have been thought sacrilegious a hundred years before, began in earnest. Very soon there were none, or, at any rate, very few of the martyrs left in their original resting-places. No one cared any longer to be buried in these deserted and melancholy spots, and so by degrees the memory of the catacombs died away ; the entrances became shut up and inaccessible ; and the knowledge even of the localities in which they were situated was entirely lost.

The process of their recovery began again at the period of the Renaissance, and has been carried much further in our own day. Only one remained always accessible, that at S. Sebastiano, preserved by the veneration for the spot where the bodies of St. Peter and St. Paul had found a temporary resting-place. This cemetery, originally the only one known as *ad catacumbas*, then came to give its name to all the rest.

It is only in our own days, and by the labours of De Rossi and his pupils, that the great wealth of evidence, a small portion of which has been cited in these chapters, has become generally available. Even now the good work is by no means completed. As the monuments of the past are once more brought to light, there may be many a fresh surprise in store for us, and many a revelation as yet undreamt of may bring into greater clearness the constant and practical faith of the early Church on this subject of the Communion of Saints.

CHAPTER VII.

Portraits and Representations.

THE monuments of the earliest Christian art include among them a number of representations of our Lord and of the Saints, concerning which it is of the greatest interest to ask the question whether any of them can be regarded as authentic, or whether all alike must be considered to be merely the pious imaginations of Christians of the period. Is there, in other words, any real and true tradition to tell us how our Lord, His blessed mother, and His Apostles appeared in the eyes of men while they were upon earth ; or have we nothing better to go upon than the attempts of Christian artists of all ages to depict them as it seemed to them to be most fitting—attempts which in the course of ages have crystallized into the conventional features which are so familiar to us at the present time ?

There is, of course, no insuperable antecedent improbability in authentic contemporary portraits having been handed down. Portrait-painting in the time of Augustus and his immediate successors at Rome was practised very extensively and with very considerable skill. Marble busts especially of this period have come down to us in great numbers ; and from them we can judge of the ability of the Roman artists to catch a likeness and to fix it in imperishable stone. The features of every emperor and of almost every great man of the early imperial period are as well known to us to-day as are those of the kings and statesmen of the eighteenth century. The paintings of the same period have almost all perished through the lapse of time, though formerly they must have existed in very great numbers. Only a few still survive, for the most part preserved by the climate and the sands of Upper Egypt. But these few are more than sufficient to show us how flourishing and widespread an art portrait-painting was in the imperial age, and at the same time to prove that its exercise was by no means limited to the capital itself. If portraits were being painted constantly and in great numbers in Upper Egypt, there is no reason why some few at least who were competent to produce a satisfactory likeness should not have been found in Jerusalem at the same period.

Nor, again, is there any theological reason why such portraits should not exist. The Mosaic prohibition against images and likenesses produced for the purpose of worship, was, as Christians saw clearly from a very early time, repealed by the very fact of the Incarnation, and no religious prejudice was felt against representations of our Lord or of the Saints. This is proved both by the writings of the anti-Nicene Fathers, and by the large numbers of such representations which do in fact exist. The Judaistic reaction which gave birth in later times to the Iconoclastic controversies was foreign to the minds of the Christians of the earliest centuries.

The Blessed Trinity.

So far, indeed, were these from regarding it as unlawful to make a representation for religious purposes of our Lord or of the Saints, that they did not even shrink from representing the Uncreated. There is, for instance, in the Lateran Museum of Christian

CHRIST AND ST. PETER

From a sarcophagus in the Lateran Museum

From Marucchi's "I Monumenti del Museo Cristiano Pio-Lateranense"

EARLIEST REPRESENTATION OF THE TRINITY

From a sarcophagus in the Lateran Museum

From Marucchi's "I Monumenti del Museo Cristiano Pio-Lateranense"
(Milan : Ulrico Hoepli)

Antiquities a sarcophagus of very great importance, which was discovered when excavations were being made, about the middle of the last century, for the construction of the new baldachino over the high altar of St. Paul's. It is of the latter part of the fourth century. Christian sarcophagi of carved stone are seldom earlier than the peace of the Church, because of the impossibility during the times of persecution of getting Christian subjects executed in pagan work-shops. In the times of persecution the sarcophagi of Christians rarely show definitely Christian ornamentation, but such pagan forms as were not objectionable had perforce to be pressed into the service.

On this sarcophagus on the right side and in the upper tier, there are three bearded figures which appear to represent the three Persons of the Blessed Trinity engaged on the creation of Eve from the side of Adam. The Eternal Father, represented as an old man with bald head and wrinkled brow, is standing behind a seat on which is a second figure with the hand raised in the act of speaking. The nude figure of Adam lies, apparently dead, on the ground, and a third figure stands beside him, with his hand on the head of a young girl. The second figure, seated and speaking, is the Eternal Word, with whom to speak is to effect and " by whom all things were made ". The third is the Holy Spirit, the hand on the head of Eve implying the work of sanctification. Thus each of the three Persons of the Blessed Trinity are represented according to his proper operation. The Word speaks and creates ; the Holy Spirit sanctifies ; the Eternal Father is present as the One Source of Deity, united in Will with the Word and the Holy Spirit.

De Rossi explains the three figures somewhat differently. He would make the seated figure to be the Eternal Father, the figure with the hand on the head of Eve to be the Word, and the one behind the throne to be the Holy Spirit. But the explanation we have given, which is that which used to be given by Professor Armellini in his lectures at the Propaganda, seems to be the better and to express more accurately the several operations of the Three Persons.

Portraits of our Lord.

The earliest representations of our Lord in the catacombs were not portraits. He is represented at first ideally, as a beautiful and beardless youth, generally under the form of the Good Shepherd. In these pictures there is, quite obviously, no attempt whatever at portraiture, nor at any kind of verisimilitude. It is an *idea* which is portrayed, not the Christ as He walked on earth. The whole treatment is conventional and cannot possibly be mistaken for anything else. It was no part of the purpose of those artists who made such pictures to present to the eyes of the faithful the actual features of the historical Christ, but only to speak to them of the beauty of His character, and of the work that He accomplished for the salvation of souls.

But here and there in the catacombs themselves, and in many specimens of the art of the earliest centuries, we do find representations of a different type. These latter are not of a merely conventional character, but certainly give the idea of an attempt to set forth an actual likeness. They do not seem to be, as a rule, of the very earliest date—the conventional type seems to be the older of the two, but some of them are perhaps as old as the second century, and there is nothing to forbid their being based on some generally accepted description of our Lord's appearance, or even on some actual portrait drawn by some person whose eyes had rested on the living features of Jesus Christ.

The Statue of Baneas.

We know from various passages in early writers that portraits of our Lord were in existence in the second century. St. Irenaeus, for instance (" Contr. Haeres," I. xxv. 6), tells us that the Carpocratian heretics possessed such, which they said were copied from a picture made by order of Pilate. These portraits fall under suspicion, if for no other reason, because they were put forward by heretics, but there was one famous example to which no taint of heresy has ever clung, and which may perhaps go back not only to the second century but even to the first. This was the famous statue of Baneas, the Caesarea Philippi of the Gospels, which was said to have been set up by Berenice of Edessa, the woman cured by our Lord of an issue of blood. We know of it chiefly from Eusebius, who speaks thus : " Since I have mentioned this city of Paneas I think I ought not to omit an account which is worthy of record for posterity. For they say that the woman with an issue of blood, who, as we learn from the sacred Gospel, received from our Saviour deliverance from her affliction, came from this place, and that her house is shown in the city, and that noteworthy memorials of the kindness of the Saviour to her remain there. For there stands upon a raised stone, by the gates of her house, a bronze image of a woman kneeling, with her hands stretched out, as if she were praying. Opposite to her stands the figure of a man made of the same material, clothed in comely fashion in a double cloak, and extending his hand towards the woman. . . . They say that this statue is an image of Jesus. It has remained to our day, so that we ourselves also saw it when we were staying in the city. Nor is it strange that those of the Gentiles who were benefited by our Saviour should have done such things, when we learn also that the likenesses of His Apostles Paul and Peter and of Christ Himself are preserved in paintings, the ancients being accustomed, as is common among the Gentiles, to pay this kind of honour to all those whom they regarded as deliverers" ("Hist. Eccl.," vii. 18).

It is clear from this passage that Eusebius himself believed that this statue actually was what it claimed to be, and it seems probable that he was right. Many have urged that it was only a statue of some Emperor, such as Hadrian, with the kneeling figure of a Province. That would be likely enough if the date was later, but in the time of Eusebius, when Christianity had only just become free, it would be very unlikely that the statue of an Emperor should have lost its identity, and should have been generally regarded as a representation of Christ. The later history of the statue confirms this idea of its genuineness. It was broken up by Julian the Apostate (Sozomen, V. xxi.), and the fragments were collected by the Christians and put into the church of the town.

It is possible that although this statue no longer survives we yet have a representation of it upon one of the sarcophagi of the Lateran Museum. Here we have a woman kneeling, much as Eusebius describes, and stretching out her hands in supplication to the figure of our Lord, who stands vested in a kind of toga, with His face in profile, looking at the suppliant towards whom He stretches out His hand. The face of our Lord is bearded, which is rare in works of this period, and gives one the idea of a portrait. This is the more remarkable because on the same sarcophagus we have another representation of Him which is quite conventional and beardless. . . . It is possible, of course, that the subject is the *Noli me tangere*, Magdalene at the feet of Jesus after His Resurrection. However, the view that it represents the group of Baneas has much to be said for it, and has been held by such men as Garucci (Storia, i. 406), De Rossi and Leclercq. It is the more probable if the further opinion be true, which is based on some expressions in Macarius Magnès, that a replica of the Baneas statue existed at Rome.

The Acheiropoieta.

If only their authenticity can be accepted, the earliest portraits of Christ and those whose likeness is most beyond dispute, will be that group of portraits on linen which claim a miraculous origin, and are hence known by the name of ACHEIROPOIETA as not being made by mortal hands. Of these there are several in existence, of which the best known is the " Veronica " at St. Peter's in Rome, the portrait preserved at St. Silvestro in Capite, the Holy Shroud at Turin and the portrait in the Sancta Sanctorum in the Lateran. Of these it is very difficult to speak with any confidence from a purely archæological point of view. Their documentary history is for the most part not very satisfactory, and this is especially true of the Holy Shroud. For the earlier centuries there is, naturally enough, no documentary evidence at all, but this could scarcely be expected for the ages of persecution. Many questions might be set at rest if these relics were subjected to a close and scientific investigation, but this has hitherto been refused, and the great care and veneration with which they are preserved make it impossible for any minute examination of their state and real character to be carried out. One thing and one thing only is clear about them and that is that the general type of the likeness of Christ which has been received from the fourth century at least, if not earlier, is to be found in all of them.

Perhaps the most remarkable of these relics is the Holy Shroud of Turin.   Its documentary history is unsatisfactory, as we have already said, and certainly lays it open to suspicion, though it is not absolutely inconsistent with its real authenticity.   But the representation of Christ which it affords is very notable.   To the ordinary eye there is little to be seen but a few brown stains, which take the general form of a human body, the actual features of the face being scarcely decipherable.   But when it was last exposed for public veneration at the time of the Eucharistic Congress of Turin in 1896, a photograph was taken of it.   The photographic negative gave a far more clear portrait than the original, and showed, what no one had hitherto suspected, that the marks on the linen are themselves, photographically speaking, negative ; that is, that the light and shade is the reverse of that which obtains in nature.   The fact is a very singular one, and it is certainly not easy to explain.   In any case, and whatever its origin may be, we have recovered from the photographic negative what amounts to a new portrait of Christ ; although itself undoubtedly of very great antiquity, which preserves the traditional likeness, and yet goes beyond any other in some characteristics of dignity and of suffering.   From an artistic point of view, and we confine ourselves to that until further information is forthcoming through a detailed examination of the relic, it is of the highest importance as a powerful conception of the suffering Christ.

The Gilded Glasses.

These form a branch of art which is almost entirely Christian and limited to the earliest centuries.   Most of them belong to the third and fourth centuries, but

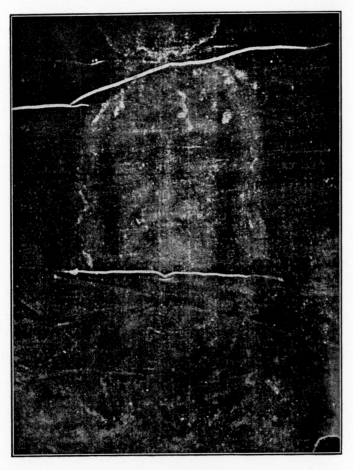

FACE OF CHRIST

From a negative photograph of the Holy Shroud

(To get the best effect the picture should be looked at from some distance)

From Vignon's " Le Linceul du Christ" (Masson et Cie)

some go back at least to the second. The manufacture
became a lost art about the end of the fourth century.
They consist of two disks of glass united in the furnace, between which is a piece of gold leaf, so treated
as to form a picture or an inscription. Very often
they seem to have formed the bases of cups, the upper
portions of which have been destroyed by time.
Sometimes they were parts of boxes or caskets made
for religious or domestic uses. It is possible even
that in some cases they were actually chalices used for
the Eucharistic service. Among the glasses of this
kind preserved in the Vatican Museum are several
which have the figure of our Lord, some with the inscription ZESVS CRISTVS. The small size of these
glasses causes the portraits shown upon them to be
also very small, but they are still quite recognizable,
and are evidently attempts at actual portraiture and
not mere conventional representations. Their principal importance in the matter of the likeness of Christ
is that they tend to prove that this likeness was not a
mere invention of later centuries, the result of the
concordant action of many artistic minds, but that it
was actually handed down by tradition all through the
years of persecution in Rome. But it is very doubtful indeed whether this evidence is strengthened or
weakened when we go on to take into consideration
what the catacombs have to teach us.

The Representations of Christ in the Catacombs.

The great majority of the representations of our
Lord which are to be found in the catacombs are, as
has already been said, of a purely conventional
character. Indeed it is extremely doubtful whether
there is any single example, earlier than the latter half
of the fourth century, which even aims at any actual

portraiture. It could hardly have been otherwise if we consider the circumstances of the case, for to paint up in large size the actual features of our Lord, supposing them to have been available, would only have been to run the risk of their defacement and insult at Pagan hands.

There is, however, if we may take Mgr. Wilpert as our guide, a certain development observable in the various representations which remain, if we take them in chronological order. In the oldest examples, which date from the first half of the second century, our Lord is represented as youthful and beardless. This is true of all the examples of the second century. In the third century we meet for the first time with the beard. It is short and the hair is long and falls on the shoulders. This older type, however, still persisted and is the one generally employed right down to the peace of the Church.

The earliest picture in the catacombs to approximate to the modern idea is to be found in Sta Domitilla and is of the second half of the fourth century. Here it seems clear that the artist is attempting a portrait, and it is of great importance for this reason.

Sir W. Wyke Bayliss, in his interesting but unconvincing book "Rex Regum," laid much stress on a small portrait in the Catacombs of St. Callixtus. It was copied by Mr. Heaphy with great care, and if we can trust the fidelity of his reproduction it would be, perhaps, the most important piece of evidence we possess. Unfortunately, however, it is impossible to test this, for the picture has now been destroyed by the joint action of the damp and of the smoke from tourists' torches. In Mr. Heaphy's drawing it certainly seems to carry back the traditional likeness at Rome to a period earlier than the peace of Constantine.

THE CHRIST OF THE CATACOMBS
From a fresco in the Catacomb of St. Callixtus
From Bayliss' "Rex Regum" (S.P.C.K.)

VIRGIN AND CHILD.   IN THE OSTRIAN CEMETERY AT ROME
From Marucchi's " Eiéments d'Archéologie" (Desclée, De Brouwer et Cie)

If we try to sum up the whole of the evidence which is available on the subject of the early representations of our Lord, we find ourselves unable to pronounce with absolute certainty how far the Church is in possession of a likeness which may be considered really authentic.   Of course, as Sir William Wyke Bayliss points out, we must distinguish carefully between the Likeness and the likenesses.   It is not a simple question of the authenticity of any single picture, but rather the question whether the similarity which underlies so many of the representations be not based on an authentic picture which is now lost, or at least upon trustworthy tradition.   Probably it is a question which we must leave undecided and which each will answer according to his own predilections. There is certainly no impossibility, rather on the other hand an antecedent probability, that some attempt should have been made to hand down features which meant so much to the world.   On the other hand the evidence is not sufficiently clear, and the difficulty of accurately dating and estimating the evidence is too great to allow of any real certainty in the matter.

Sir W. Wyke Bayliss notes one little point which is of considerable interest.   There must be at least two separate exemplars from which the traditional likenesses of our Lord in the East and in the West have been respectively derived.   A very simple criterion enables one to say with practical certainty whether any particular example of ancient date is of Eastern or of Roman origin.   If it is from the East it will show the hair with a small lock detached and falling in the centre of the forehead.   If it is Roman in origin the hair will be divided evenly over the forehead with no detached lock at all.   This minute detail, which is carefully and conscientiously kept to, certainly seems to show that the artist believed himself to be following an authentic likeness, which he was bound to hand on intact, and with which he had no right to take even the slightest liberty.   There can be little doubt that at the time of Constantine there were pictures in existence which were believed to be authentic, and that these served as the models on which those great pictures in mosaic were built up in the basilicas which fixed the tradition of the likeness of Christ for all men and for all time.   The only real question is how far these early pictures were themselves trustworthy or only imaginative, and that, as we have said, is a question on which we have not, at present, sufficient evidence to enable us to give a really decisive answer.

Representations of our Blessed Lady.

When we turn next to the representations of our Blessed Lady which have come down to us from the early centuries, we find the conditions of the problem are precisely the opposite to those which obtain in the case of our Lord.   It is very rare to find any representation of our Lady, either alone or with the Holy Child, on the small objects of devotion which have survived.   On the other hand, there are several large paintings in the catacombs which deal with this subject and call for careful attention.

The most important is to be found in the Catacomb of Sta Priscilla, and is of very early date.   In the centre of the composition is a figure of the Good Shepherd, with a family group on the left.   On the right is the Holy Virgin, seated and holding the Infant Jesus at her breast.   Before her stands an upright figure who seems to represent a Prophet, and who is pointing to a star above her head.[1]   The style of the whole is classic in character, and the date can hardly be put later than the opening years of the second

[1] See Plate opposite p. 52.

century. There are two or three other pictures of our Lady in the same catacomb, but they are of less importance.

In the Catacomb of St. Domitilla is a painting of the third century which represents the Epiphany. Our Lady is in the centre, veiled and seated upon a chair, with the Holy Child upon her knees. The wise men are four in number and bring their gifts on trays on either side. In another similar scene a little later in date which has survived in the Catacomb of S. Peter and Marcellinus the wise men are only two.

In the Ostrian Cemetery in an arcosolium over a tomb is a very famous picture of our Lady, which is the first which does not form part of a historical scene. It is of the fourth century and later than Constantine as may be seen by the monogram on each side. The face of the Virgin looks straight out of the picture and the Holy Child is in the centre on her breast. It is the prototype of all those pictures of our Lady in the same position which were common from this time down to the Renaissance and still survive in the eikons of the Eastern Church.

The importance of these frescoes of the catacombs is very considerable from a doctrinal point of view. They prove that honour was paid to our Blessed Lady, at a period long before the Council of Ephesus. But the faces of the various representations do not seem to be portraits. They do not lead us to think that the early Church possessed any likeness of our Lady which was held to be authentic. The features are conventional and without character, and there is no common likeness, as is so marked in the case of our Lord.

Against this conclusion, however, may be quoted the various paintings of our Lady which are preserved in different places, and which are said to be from the hand of St. Luke. The most famous of these is, perhaps, the one in Sta Maria Maggiore, the history of which can be traced back at least to the ninth century. But no one of these pictures can possibly go back behind the Byzantine period, as is clear from the style of the art and details of the painting, nor is there any reason to think they were based to any great extent on earlier examples. On the whole, therefore, it must be admitted that there is no reason to think that any authentic likeness of our Blessed Lady has been preserved, although the earliest of the pictures which represent her in the catacombs may well have been painted by one who, so far as age is concerned, might have seen her in the flesh.

The Apostles.

There can, however, be no doubt at all that we do possess actual portraits of two at least of the Apostles St. Peter and St. Paul. We owe this, no doubt, to the fact that, while the other Apostles laboured in distant countries and never visited the capital at all, St. Peter and St. Paul were well known in Rome itself. The type of face assigned to each of these Apostles is quite clear and distinct and never varies. We have examples on the gilded glasses, on medals and plaques, as well as on the walls of the catacombs.

The earliest and at the same time one of the most distinct of these representations of the two great Apostles is to be found in a medallion which was discovered in the Cemetery of Domitilla, and is now in the Vatican Museum. St. Peter appears with short curling hair and beard and features which are strongly marked, and those of a man who worked with his hands. The hair and beard in the catacomb pictures are grey. St. Paul is of a more aristocratic and intel-

ST. PETER AND ST. PAUL
From a medallion of the Second Century in the Vatican

DANIEL IN THE LIONS' DEN
From a sarcophagus in the Lateran Museum. From Marucchi's " I Monumenti del Museo Cristiano Pio-Lateranense" (Milan : Ulrico Hoepli)

lectual type, somewhat bald and with a beard long and
pointed. The work of the medallion is of the second
century.

So familiar were the Christians of Rome with the
features of these two great Apostles that it was not
necessary to put their names to show who was represented. Every one knew their appearance and could
recognize them at once. So again, when it was
desired to emphasize for doctrinal purposes the application of some scene of Old Testament history and
to bring out the symbolism in connexion with
Christian teaching, it was not necessary to do more
than to give the familiar features of St. Peter to the
representation of an Old Testament character. Reference has already been made to this, but we repeat
once more what we have said. Let us suppose that
the scene depicted was Moses striking the rock, or
else receiving from God the Tables of the Law. The
application desired to be made was that as Moses
gave water to the thirsty Israelites so also were
Christians to draw the refreshments of the Sacraments
from the Apostolic ministry. Or, again, that as
Moses was the Lawgiver of the Old Testament, sent
and commissioned by God, so also must we look
for the New Law to the teaching of the Apostles sent
by Christ. It was quite sufficient, in order to bring
this teaching home to the mind of every Christian of
the first centuries, to depict Moses with the face of
Peter. So familiar was that face to all, so unmistak-
able were its well-known features, that none could
miss the lesson which was meant to be conveyed.

Of the other Apostles and of the leading figures of
the Church of the first century, we do not seem to have
any portraits. The gilded glasses provide us with
representations of St. John, St. Linus, and others, but
in the absence of a sufficient number of examples to

compare with one another it is not possible to say whether any of these are intended as actual portraits. Of St. Peter and St. Paul there can be no reasonable doubt at all, but with them we must be content. There is no certainty, scarcely even a probability, that we possess any authentic likeness of any other one from among the first generation of Christians either at Rome or in any other part of the Empire.

PART III.

CHAPTER I.

Christian Edifices before Constantine.

THE earliest of all the edifices consecrated to Christian worship was that upper room in Jerusalem, where our Lord had instituted the Holy Eucharist, and where on the day of Pentecost the Holy Ghost had come down upon the assembled Apostles. A place with such memories could not possibly be neglected, and it is without surprise, therefore, that we find that the local tradition of Jerusalem has preserved the identity of this sacred spot. This upper room, capable as it was, apparently, of accommodating at least 120 persons, became, naturally enough, the central and perhaps the only place of meeting of the little band of Christians in Jerusalem before the dispersion of the Apostles. They went daily to the Temple for the prayers of their nation, and returned "to break bread," κατ᾽ οἶκον, not from house to house as the "Authorized Version" translates the phrase, nor even "at home," but rather "in the house"; in that house and place, that is to say, which had been originally consecrated by the institution of the Blessed Sacrament, and which now remained the normal centre of its administration.

The house, lying as it did on the outskirts of

Jerusalem, survived, so again tradition informs us, the destruction of the siege of Jerusalem, in A.D. 70, and it was still in being and still preserved its essential characteristic of an upper room when St. Epiphanius wrote about A.D. 380.[1] It still survives and still is an upper chamber, but is now in the hands of the infidels. Moreover, such changes have been made in the lapse of ages that it is impossible to make any certain deductions from its present form. Outside of Jerusalem when the Apostles were scattered over the world, preaching the gospel, we should naturally expect to find them preserving in the main this original plan of action. The appeal was everywhere made first to the Jews; every possible use was made of the existing organization of the Jewish body, for the time of definitive separation had not yet come, and the hope was still alive that the Jewish nation as a whole might yet accept the gospel message. But there must always in each place have been some one chosen spot where Christians could meet for their own special devotions; where, as in Jerusalem, they could "break bread in the house," besides using the public worship of their nation.

We can follow the process in detail in the history of St. Paul as narrated in the Acts. The missionary work of the Church was conducted for the most part in the Synagogues. Everywhere we find him as soon as he arrived in a new town, going straight to the Synagogue, and there delivering his message as a Jew to Jews. But at the same time we are aware that there is another kind of religious work being carried on, and this not in the Synagogue, nor in any public place, but in the privacy of a convert's house. At Troas, for instance, this private assembly was held on the third floor (εἰς τὸ ὑπερῷον, Acts xx. 6-9); at Rome St. Paul sends salutations to Aquila and Priscilla "and

---

[1] "De Mens.," xiv.; cf. Cyr. Hier., "Catech.," vi.

the church that is in their house" (Rom. XVI. 5); at
Colosse, it is in the house of Nymphe (Col. IV. 15);
at Ephesus, besides the church in the house of Aquila
(1 Cor. XVI. 19), we find that a public hall has been taken
for missionary work, and St. Paul disputes daily in the
schola of one Tyrannus (Acts XIX. 9).

Private Oratories.

Here then we have the real origin of the Christian
churches of later date. It begins with private oratories
sheltered by the rights of private property. If we
are to get any idea of these places now, it can only
be by examining the general plan of a Roman house,
and forming our ideas as to the most usual disposition
which would be made for these purposes. Individual
cases must, of course, have varied widely, but the
general type was pretty constant, and from it we may
gather some ideas of value.

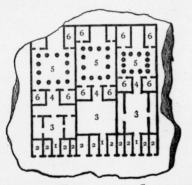

ROMAN HOUSES AS SHOWN ON THE CAPITOLINE PLAN.
(*From Sir W. Smith's "Greek and Roman Antiquities," John Murray.*)

The arrangement of a Roman house was mainly on
a single floor, though sometimes in crowded localities
upper stories were added. It was entered from the

street by a passage which led into the *atrium*, the more
public part of the house. From this access could be
obtained to the peristyle, an inner courtyard surrounded by pillars, round which were built the private
rooms of the family. At the far end of the peristyle
was usually a larger chamber, the *oecus* or *tablinum*,
which served as a private reception room for the
owner of the house.

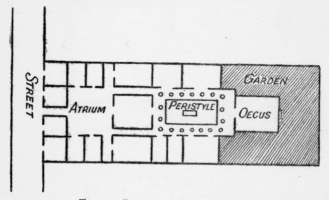

TYPICAL PLAN OF A ROMAN HOUSE.

If we take these main features, neglecting the sub-
sidiary arrangements, which varied in every way, we
shall see that if the owner of such a house as this were
called upon to make provision for a meeting of Christians for the purpose of worship, he would have found
his premises admirably adapted for this object. The
guests would naturally be admitted into the inner portion of the house, for fear of interruption. The *oecus*
would be the natural place for the officiating clergy,
and so forth, and the peristyle would afford accommodation for a large number of worshippers. If that was
the arrangement made, we can already recognize the
germ of our later plans. We have the large oblong

space for the ordinary worshippers, and we have also the smaller apartment, similarly oblong in form and separated from the other by an arch, which forms the chancel. It is precisely and identically the plan which is so familiar to us in the north as that of our oldest churches.

TYPICAL PLAN OF AN ANCIENT ENGLISH CHURCH.

The Ecclesia Domestica.

Only two oratories certainly earlier than the time of Constantine are known to exist in Rome. One of these at Sta Prisca was discovered in 1776 and has again been lost. We have no certain record of its shape. The other was recently found near the Via Venti Settembre, and is rectangular and apseless with a vine-patterned mosaic pavement enclosing an altar compartment with symbolic cross and fishes.[1]

Two passages in the " Clementine Recognitions " are of special interest. Although some of this document is to be assigned to a later date, the ground plan of it is very early indeed, and of considerable value. We read in it that at Tripoli, when the Apostle Peter was there, and great numbers were converted through his preaching, a certain prominent citizen named Maro

[1] Frothingham, " Amer. Journal of Archæology," 1903, p. 77.

offered a spacious hall in his house capable of holding more than 500 persons. There was also a garden adjoining which could accommodate even more. So again at Antioch under similar circumstances one Theophilus, a chief noble of the place, " consecrated the great hall of his house under the name of a church," and Peter's chair was placed there.[1]

The passages are interesting whatever may be their exact authority, because they put before us an instance of what was undoubtedly happening frequently during the years of persecution, and constitutes a further step in the development of a church. As the number of Christians increased, and got beyond the small circle of individual friends of single proprietors, the private house obviously became unsuitable for public worship. It might be tolerated as being inevitable, on the ground that no more fixed and adequate arrangements were possible on account of persecution ; but it is evident that more general accommodation would have to be provided where it was possible. So there grew up the *ecclesia domestica* as we meet with it in the second and third centuries ; a real church, though held in what was externally a private house. Certain houses were bought, or were handed over by their owners for the express purpose of being used as churches. Henceforth they were occupied, not by private individuals, but by the priests who served the church. Probably they still preserved the appearance of private houses, internally as well as externally, so as to avoid attracting attention and in order to disarm all suspicion. The priests lived in the more private rooms of the house, and the peristyle and *oecus* as usual formed the church.

We have several records of private houses which were turned into churches in this way. The house

[1] " Clem. Recogn.," iv. 6 and x. 71.

of Clement, one of the earliest popes, became the church which bears his name. The house of Pudens apparently bears the same relation to Sta Pudenziana, and that of Aquila on the Aventine to the church of Sta Prisca. In later times we find Lucina giving her house for the purpose, and it becomes the church of S. Marcello in Corso.[1] So also in the Acts of St. Cecilia, which are rather late but based on earlier material, we are told that as the saint lay dying she handed over her house to the bishop that it might be made into a church.[2] The pipes which belonged to the baths in that house may still be seen in the Church of Sta Cecilia in Trastevere.

A very curious document, which is printed in the appendix to Vol. IX. of Migne's edition of St. Augustine ("P.L.," xliii. p. 794), gives us an account of a domiciliary visit paid during the course of the persecution of Diocletian to such an *ecclesia domestica* as we have described at Cirta in Africa. The Roman Magistrate Felix comes to "the house in which the Christians were wont to meet," evidently a place which was perfectly well known, and finds there Paul the Bishop and others of the clergy. He orders the Bishop to produce the Scriptures and anything else he possessed, so as to obey the law which ordered these to be destroyed. The Bishop replies that these were in the hands of the lectors, and on being further asked to produce the lectors, answers that their names were well known to the authorities, which is not disputed. A large number of clergy, priests, deacons, subdeacons, and fossors are mentioned as being present, and an inventory was taken of the things which were produced, including two cups of gold, six of silver, six silver ewers, seven silver lamps, two candelabra with branches,

[1] *Acta Marcelli.*
[2] *Acta Ceciliae.*

seven short bronze candlesticks, and eleven lamps. There was also a large quantity of clothing for both men and women, which, it has been suggested, was used by poorer Christians when they came to the Agape, after the manner of the wedding garment in the parable. Afterwards search was made in the library, but apparently there had been time to hide the books, for the cases were found empty. Then the triclinium, or dining-room, was searched, and here four jars and six vases were found. A large number of codices were afterwards discovered by visits to other houses, and these were all destroyed. The whole document is full of interest, as showing just what was happening at the time all over the Empire.

The Scholae.

We have seen how at Corinth, even in apostolic times, the needs of the young Christian community were such that no private house could fulfil the

TYPICAL FORMS OF ROMAN SCHOLAE.

purpose, and a public hall or *schola* had to be acquired. It is likely enough that a similar need in other places and later times was satisfied in like fashion. These

type of the Christian Church, the influence of these *cellae* does not seem to have been great, and it is hardly worth our while, consequently, to pursue the subject much further.

In Rome itself there is not a single church, properly so called, which is of this form. Within the city and throughout Italy the basilican type has carried all before it. But there are a certain number of very ancient churches in the more remote parts of the Empire which are not altogether of the basilican type, and do not seem to have derived their plan from purely domestic architecture. These churches are for the most part not very large and are not divided up by pillars into aisles. They are generally simple rectangles with a large apse at the end, taking up the whole of that side of the rectangle. There are, for instance, two very remarkable churches of this form at Surp Garabed in Cappadocia,[1] entirely excavated in the solid rock and adjoining one another. There are other examples at Babouda,[2] between Damascus and Aleppo, and at Chagque [3] to the south-east of Damascus. The shape of all these is exactly that of the *schola* or *cella* as we find it at Pompeii, and on the plans of ancient Rome, and it may well be that such of the Christian Churches of pre-Constantinian date as were derived from this origin, rather than from the *ecclesia domestica*, were generally of this form.

Chapels at the Catacombs.

Besides the *cella* or *schola* above ground at the cemeteries there were chapels underground, in the catacombs themselves, generally at the shrines of the martyrs, and from these again there is much to be learnt as to

---

[1] Texier and Pullan, " Byzantine Architecture," p. 39.
[2] " Syrie Centrale," par le Comte de Vogüé.
[3] *Idem.*

the arrangements thought essential for Divine worship in the earliest ages. Clearly we have to do here not with the luxuries of worship, but with the barest necessaries. For the most part they are simple *cubicula*, rather larger than the others, and that is all. The famous crypt of the Popes at St. Callixtus, where so many of the Popes of the third century are buried, may serve as an example. Here we have a simple rectangular chamber, with no liturgical division of any kind, at one end of which, apparently, the altar was erected. Where the conditions were so severely limited, very little could be done. The Church had to worship in these places, not indeed as she would, but as she found it possible. Their interest is extreme, but they have not much to teach us as to the course and direction of liturgical development.

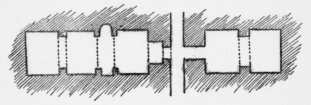

CHAPEL AT THE OSTRIAN CEMETERY.

There is, however, in another catacomb, that of the Ostrian cemetery on the Via Nomentana, a much more detailed arrangement for Divine worship. A chapel of some size has been formed by connecting, so as to make into a single elongated chamber, a number of the small cubicula which are so frequent. There are five of these altogether, three in front of and two behind the passage by which access is obtained. The two behind were given up to the women; we have provision for the separation of the sexes even here. The next two are similarly for the men, while the remaining one at the extreme end is for the clergy. The Bishop's throne, cut in the rock, is against the back wall, facing down the chapel, and the seats for the presbyters are on either side. A portable altar, apparently, was placed in front of him. A good deal of trouble has been taken to give the whole place an architectural effect, by cutting pilasters at the side and so forth, and places are provided for lamps. The interest of the place is great because we see that here, in spite of the difficulties of the situation, a real attempt has been made to provide proper accommodation as it was then conceived of. We may be sure that in oratories above ground, when things were peaceable and such oratories were able to exist, all these distinctions would have been held absolutely necessary. In any reconstruction of the arrangements of such an oratory, we should have to provide separate accommodation for the two sexes, as well as a special place, well divided off from the rest of the oratory, for the Bishop and his clergy.

The Basilica.

So far, in our search for the various elements out of which the traditional arrangements of our churches have come into existence, the structure of the Roman house has been by far the most important. The other element, the *schola* and the subterranean crypt might almost be neglected. But in the arrangements of certain large Roman houses, there was a peculiarity which is of higher importance than anything to which we have as yet drawn attention in its influence upon the form ultimately taken by Christian churches. This is the private *basilica*, or great hall of a Roman palace, which, according to Vitruvius, was a constant feature of these buildings, and was constructed accord-

[1] Vitruvius, " De archit." vi. v. 8.

13

ing to the same general rules as the public basilicas which were used as law courts and exchanges. We have the remains of a private basilica of this kind in the palace of Domitian on the Palatine. It was used for giving audiences to clients and for the decision of causes which were brought before the Emperor personally, and doubtless many a Christian has stood and been judged within it. Such private basilicas differed from the oecus of an ordinary house mainly by the

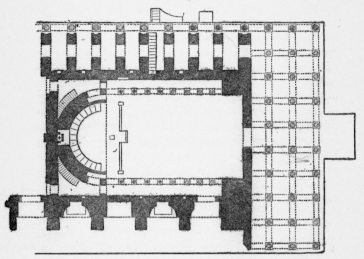

PLAN OF THE BASILICA JULIA, on the Palatine at Rome.

addition of an apse at the end, and, if this was rendered necessary because of the greater size, of pillars down each side to help to support the roof. The tablinum or oecus was an ordinary room in which the host received his guests and moved about among them. The basilica on the contrary was a hall to which the prince or noble went to receive his clients and to hear their causes. Hence there was a necessity for the apse to form a focus to dominate the whole and to make a fitting place for the throne of the prince when sitting as judge.

After the peace of the Church, when Christians were free to build churches as they wished, the basilica type became almost universal in the West. Christian imaginations were captured by the gift by Constantine to Pope Zephyrinus of the Lateran Palace, whose basilica became the cathedral of Rome and set the pattern for almost all future churches in the West. But all this belongs to a later period than that which we are now discussing, and before Constantine handed over the Lateran, the basilica type of church seems to have been very rare, though not perhaps absolutely unknown.

There cannot have been enough Christians of exalted position at any time to make the use of basilicas of this kind at all common during the ages of persecution. But we have a few instances of the use of the word, and it is not impossible that in one or two great houses in Rome or elsewhere such basilicas were actually used for Christian worship. Their suitability for such a purpose was remarkable. The throne of the prince, situated at the farthest point of the apse, naturally lent itself for the bishop or presiding officer, and the seats of the assessors which lined the apse on either side of the throne were equally suitable for the assisting clergy. It is the exact arrangement which we find in the Cœmeterium Ostrianum and which became the normal arrangement of the Christian Church for many centuries.

General Results.

We may sum up the results of our investigations concerning the ecclesiastical buildings in use during the ages of persecution somewhat as follows: The Christians met first in private houses and seldom had

13 *

buildings of their own apart from these. The usual thing, when it was decided to set apart a particular building as a semi-public oratory, was to utilize an ordinary house for the purpose, allowing the bishop or the priest, as the case might be, to live in the house. He will have passed, so far as the outside world was concerned, as an ordinary tenant, and probably used the peristyle and tablinum, or whatever other part of the house was most suitable, for the purposes of the public meeting. Accordingly the idea of a church which was prevalent in these centuries was that of a large oblong hall, with a second and smaller oblong sanctuary separated from the great hall by an arch. Within the bounds of the Empire of Constantine, as we shall see, this primitive ideal came to be superseded by another drawn from the basilica, but in some countries where the Roman influence was weak in the fourth and fifth centuries, such as Ireland and Britain and other parts of the North, the basilican type never succeeded in establishing itself, and the square east end of our churches even at the present time preserves the memory of the earliest type of Christian church derived from the conditions of the Roman house of the period.

In the later part of the third century and the beginning of the fourth, especially in the period of comparative peace which intervened between the persecutions of Decius and Valerius and that of Diocletian, there can be no doubt that edifices formally given over to Christian worship were rising everywhere. Eusebius would have had no motive for exaggeration, and he tells us that they were very numerous. "Who could describe," he asks, "the vast crowds of those who came daily to religious worship, or the number of churches in every town?"[1] The old churches, he

[1] "Hist. eccl.," viii. 3.

goes on to say, had grown too small, and everywhere new and vast churches were rising up.   Other
testimonies are completely in accord with this, and it
is evident that at this period the picture commonly
drawn of the worship carried on with difficulty in the
depths of the catacombs and other similar places, however true it may be for the comparatively few years of
active persecution, does not apply at all to the longer
years of truce between Church and State.   St. Optatus
of Milevis counted forty Christian churches at Rome
at this time, and we know that in the middle of
the third century, under Pope St. Cornelius, Rome
already possessed at least eighty-six priests.   But
of all these churches absolutely nothing remains
to us.   Probably they were of light construction,
and it may be that they were, after all, little
more than private houses, but in any case the
order of Diocletian that they were all to be razed
and levelled with the ground seems to have swept
them all out of existence.   There is scarcely a single
building anywhere surviving, of which we can say with
certainty that it was used for Christian worship before
the time of Constantine, though no doubt many are
built on sites which were those of earlier churches.
We remain, therefore, absolutely without any trustworthy evidence as to the size, the shape, or the internal arrangements of these churches.[1]

A passage of Eusebius[2] brings before us vividly
enough the kind of destruction that was going on everywhere under Diocletian.   He is telling of the ruin of

[1] From two descriptions of churches of the pre-Constantinian
period which have come down to us, in the " Didascalia Apostolorum "
and the " Testamentum Domini," we should conclude that they were
usually single naved and without aisles.

[2] " Hist. eccl.," viii. 2 ; cf. " De Mart. Pal.," i. 436, and Lactantius
" de mort, Persec.," xii.

the church of Nicomedia within sight of the Imperial
Palace. It was the last day of the Terminalia (the
seventh of the calends of March). In obedience to the
Imperial order, the Roman soldiers burst into the
Christian church, breaking down its gates. They
searched everywhere for the image of God, so little
as this even then was known of Christianity; burnt
the books of the Scriptures and of the liturgies; everything was given over to pillage and destruction. The
Emperors stood in the palace and watched what was
going on. They discussed the question whether the
building should be set on fire. But Diocletian was
against this, he feared that the flames would spread
and that other structures would be involved. His
opinion prevailed, but the building was not therefore
spared. The soldiers set to work with axes and crow-
bars, and in a very few hours the whole was destroyed.
Nothing remained to show where the church had stood
except only the foundations upon which it had been
built.

Everywhere all over the Empire the same tale of
destruction was going on. At Cirta we have already
told the story of the visit of the magistrates. The
destruction of the church no doubt followed though it
is not recorded. The persecutors could destroy the
churches, they could not touch the ecclesiastical organization under which those churches were worked.
Everywhere the hierarchic arrangement of dioceses and
patriarchates survived the storm. Within each diocese,
too, there must have been a detailed organization of
priests and of other clergy, and this, too, continued
unchanged. Rome itself was by this time minutely
organized for ecclesiastical purposes, and we will bring
our account of the period of persecution to an end by
giving a sketch of this organization, as we find it at
this period.

The Tituli.

The earliest notice we have of such an organization is in the "Liber Pontificalis". St. Fabian (250), we read there, "divided the regions among the deacons". There were seven deacons at Rome (the number is still preserved in that of the Cardinal Deacons of the Sacred College), and to each was assigned a "region," made up, roughly speaking, of two of the fourteen civil regions, though the arrangement allowed of certain exceptions.

Each region included a certain number of *tituli*, or "titles". These were the oldest churches in the city, and of them in the third century there were twenty-five. The reason why this name of "title" was given to the churches is generally considered uncertain. A number of very unsatisfactory suggestions were made by Baronius, who has been followed by most writers since. Certainly the name is exceedingly ancient, and dates from the very earliest age of the Church. The present author, in another work, published some twelve years ago, suggested a new derivation which seemed to him less unsatisfactory, and he would now bring it forward once again, with some additional evidence.

The word *titulus* in the Latin of the fourth century denoted among other things a memorial pillar, the Greek *Stele*, or Roman *Cippus*.

Thus, in Genesis XXVIII. 18 in the Vulgate, it is used of the stone which Jacob set up, after his dream at Bethel, *erexit in titulum*, pouring oil upon it. Similarly in the *Itinera* of the early Palestine pilgrims we find that Adamnan saw at Bethlehem the *titulus* which Jacob had set up over Rachel's grave, while an earlier pilgrim still, St. Sylvia, expresses her disappointment that the *titulus* of Lot's wife was no longer visible. Apparently the use of the word in Genesis XXVIII. 18

goes back behind the Vulgate to some form of the *Itala*, for both St. Augustine and St. Jerome quote the passage using this word. The only text of this portion of the *Itala* which survives, namely, the Lyons MS., does not have the word, but says *posuerat eum stantem*.

In Rome itself the idea of a shrine of a saint, which is pretty much what the word *titulus* seems to have meant originally, naturally connected itself with the idea of an altar, through the custom of using the tombs of the saints as altars which had grown up in the catacombs. So here we find a local and derived meaning of " altar " pure and simple ; denoting, apparently, a fixed altar of stone, in contradistinction to the wooden and portable altars, the use of which was rendered necessary by persecution. Sulpitius Severus (" Hist." i. 8) quotes the passage in Genesis, and clearly understands the word *titulus* to be simply the equivalent of "altar," for he says that Jacob promised, if he prospered, that the stone he set up, *titulum sibi domus Dei futurum*—"should be the altar of a future church"; a passage which has puzzled many commentators. Another instance of the use of the word in this sense of altar may be found in the life of St. Theofrid. *Ipse ante venerandum Beati Petri titulum in oratione est prostratus*—" He prostrated himself in prayer before the *altar* of Blessed Peter ". Next it came to mean the part about the altar, the *presbytery*, or sanctuary. In this sense it is used continually by Leo Marsicanus in the " Chronicle of Cassino," about the eleventh century. *In Ecclesia autem titulum cum confessione sua construxit.*[1] Here we might still take it to mean the altar only were it not that the same writer in another place mentions that there were six long and four round windows *in titulo*, and two in the centre apse, and others in the

[1] " Vita St. Theofridi Aff."

nave.[1] But long before this date it had acquired its final sense in Rome itself, and is used for the whole Church ; not, however, for every Church, but for those only which possessed parochial rights.[2]

The first person who is recorded to have instituted parishes of this kind is Pope Evaristus in the third century, but the authority is somewhat doubtful, and the earliest real authority is the Acts of the Roman Council of 499. At that time it applied to twenty-eight churches, of which almost all remain to the present time. The list is as follows : " Titulus Praxedis, Vestinae (St. Vitalis), St. Cecilia, Pammachii, Byzantis (SS. John and Paul), Clementis, Julii, Calixti (St. Maria in Trastevere), Chrysogoni, Pudentis, S. Sabinae, Equitii (St. Martino ai Monti), Damasi (S. Lorenzo in Damaso), Matthei (now SS. Pietro e Marcellino), Aemilianae, Eusebii, Tigridis, Crescentiani (S. Sisto), Nicomedis (unknown), Cyriaci (now transferred to St. Maria in Via Lata), S. Susannae, Gaii, Romani (doubtful), SS. Apostolorum, Eudoxiae (S. Pietro Vincula), Fasciolae (SS. Nereo e Achilleo), S. Priscae, S. Marcelli, Lucinae (S. Lorenzo in Lucina), Marci, Pallacinae. The original number before the peace of the Church was twenty-five. Three had been added in the fourth and fifth centuries, viz. SS. John and Paul, S. Lorenzo in Damaso, and another. The others were the original churches of the times of persecution, and we may suppose were for the most part at first private houses permanently used as churches, and with duly consecrated and permanent altars. They were probably all, or at least most of them, destroyed in the persecution of Diocletian, and rebuilt again after the peace of the Church. It may be noticed that they are all in the suburbs of Rome ;

---

[1] " Chron. Cass.," ii. 3-7 ; Migne, " P.L.," vol. 173, p. 586.
[2] *Ibid.* p. 747.

at least none are in the central part, which afterwards
had so many round the Forum. Nor are any in
buildings which have been taken over from the pagans;
the time for this had not yet come, although from the
same lists of the signatories of the Council of 499 we
see that the deacons had their offices already in buildings of this kind, in the *Templum sacrae Urbis* (SS.
Cosmas and Damian, and in the *horrea* or public
barns (St. Maria in Cosmedin[1]).

At a later date the parish organization of Rome
increased largely. The remains of the old system,
however, can still be traced in the College of Cardinals
with their "titular" churches; not, as is commonly
supposed, churches from which they take their titles,
but rather parochial churches of which they are, in
theory, the parish priests. The deaconries survive
also in like manner, and are held by the "Cardinal
Deacons". Their number is, however, no longer
strictly limited to seven.

[1] Cf. Duchesne, "Les titres presbyteraux," Mélanges de l'Ecole
Fr. 1887.

CHAPTER II.

The Basilicas and the Development of Church Architecture.

WE have seen in the last chapter that there were certainly Christian churches set apart for Divine worship, already existing everywhere before the end of the time of persecution. Such churches, we concluded, were probably for the most part ordinary houses, given up to this one purpose, and perhaps specially adapted for that end by internal alterations. The word *basilica* does already occur in describing these edifices, and it is possible that here and there private basilicas in large houses may have been used as churches, but this cannot have been common, and everything leads us to believe that the pre-Constantinian churches were small and square-ended for the most part, not having as yet the basilican form or possessed of an apse at the western end.

In the year 312 an event took place, the importance of which can hardly be exaggerated in the history of church architecture. Constantine handed over to the Christians the palace and basilica of the Lateran to serve as the residence of the Pope St. Zephyrinus, and to be the cathedral church of Rome. The basilica seems not to have been wholly rebuilt, but simply refitted to prepare it for its new use. St. Jerome[1] speaks

[1] " Ep.," lxxiii.

of it as *basilica quondam Laterani*, and the passage in
the "Liber Pontificalis" which records the donation
and the consecration of the church does not say that
it was actually built at this time.

As so often happens when a great forward step is
taken in architecture, the acquisition of this great hall,
probably of exceptional size and grandeur for a private
basilica, set the type for the churches so many of
which were so soon to be erected. Just as Justinian's
great church of St. Sophia at Constantinople set the
form, first for all the smaller churches of the East, and
afterwards, since the Conquest, for all the mosques of
the Turkish world, so did the basilica of the Lateran
set the type for many centuries for all the churches of
the Western Empire, and wherever Roman influence
was paramount.

The course of ages has made so much alteration in
this most important church that it is hard to say just
what was its size and shape in its original condition.
It can hardly have been so large in its original state
as at present, and probably it was greatly enlarged and
practically rebuilt in the fifth century by the Consul
Flavius Felix. The provision of the transverse nave,
for reasons which we shall see presently, must be set
down to this period and not to the original building.
The position of the altar in every church of the Constantinian period seems to have been on the chord of
the apse, just in front of the bishop's throne, and such
arrangements as transverse naves are all of later development.

The general type of the basilica is at first quite
constant, and is completely accounted for if we may
suppose that in the Lateran Palace the basilica occupied
the position of the tablinum or oecus of an ordinary
house. The plan of Old St. Peter's or S. Clemente,
or of S. Ambrogio at Milan, illustrates the point.

The basilica itself takes the place of the peristyle, and the apse succeeds to the tablinum. The atrium preserves its name, and is kept as an open forecourt, surrounded sometimes with pillars making a kind of cloister, through which the church is approached. The *impluvium* or fountain, which was usually found in the atrium of a Roman house, kept its place in the centre of the atrium of the basilica. The transition is by no means abrupt from the *ecclesia domestica* of the earlier time to the great basilicas of the centuries that follow. Even the memory of the pillars which were returned along the side of the peristyle farthest from the tablinum survived. We find pillars thus returned along the eastern side of many basilicas of the earliest date, although they seem to serve no special purpose. It was so, for instance, in the lower church at S. Clemente; in the Deir el Adra, a rock-cut church of the fourth century on the Nile; at Sta Agnese fuori le mura, and in the cathedral, now destroyed, at Messina.

Four great basilicas were erected by Constantine in Rome itself, besides the Lateran and those which he built at Jerusalem and Bethlehem, at Tyre and in Constantinople. All the four at Rome were outside the walls and over the tombs of the martyrs. They differed from one another chiefly in the number of aisles. St. Peter's, by far the largest of all, had five aisles, the others at the Lateran, Sta Agnese, S. Lorenzo, and St. Paul's had only three. Sta Agnese and S. Lorenzo, probably because the great depths to which they were excavated made this arrangement convenient, had upper galleries over the aisles. The roofing of all was by means of wooden beams carried transversely.

There is no reason to think that in making the church of St. Paul so much smaller and less important than that of St. Peter, or indeed than those of

Sta Agnese and S. Lorenzo, Constantine meant in any
way to depreciate or show little honour to the great
Apostle of the Gentiles.   In his time two canons were
always adhered to at Rome in building these churches,
in spite of every difficulty in the way.   The altar was
always placed over the tomb, and the church always
ran to the eastward of the altar, so that the celebrant
standing behind the altar, faced down the church.
The nature of the locality in which St. Paul was
buried made the creation of a large church impossible
if these rules were to be kept to.   The tomb lay just
west of the great road that ran from Rome to the
port of Ostia.   Since the road could not easily be
changed, it was only possible to build a very small
church.

But the church of St. Paul was not long allowed to
remain in this primitive condition.   In the year 386
it was determined to rebuild it, and to enlarge it in
the only way in which this could possibly be done,
by reversing its orientation.   The tomb and the altar
above it were left undisturbed.   A great arch was
raised above the altar, and westwards from that point
a vast church of five aisles was built, rivalling both in
size and magnificence the sister church of St. Peter.
East of the great arch, the whole space which had
been filled by the old church, besides a good deal more
to right and to left of it, was occupied by a vast transverse nave, at right angles to that of the great nave
and of similar height, and out of this again opened the
tribune or apse with the pontifical throne and the
semicircular benches for the clergy.   The exigences
of the situation had thus been met by two striking
innovations, each of which has been fertile in further
consequences in the development of church architecture,
namely, the introduction of the cross or tranverse nave,
and the reversal of the hitherto universally accepted

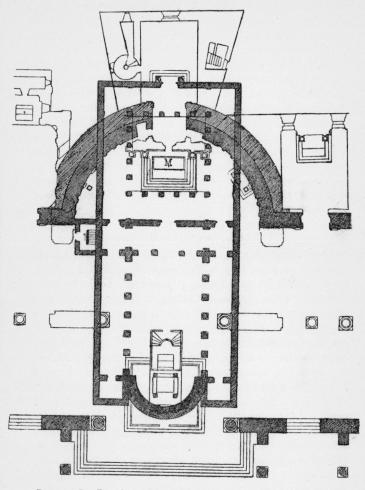

PLAN OF ST. PAUL'S AT ROME, illustrating the relation of the earlier and later churches.

relations between the altar and the church in which it stood. The transverse nave came into existence through what we may almost call the accidental circumstance that it was necessary to reverse the direction of the basilica of St. Paul, without either disturbing the tomb in which the Apostle lay, or allowing any portion of the ground already consecrated for the existing church to revert to secular uses. There may, or may not, have been the further idea of reproducing the form of the cross in the plan of the new basilica ; but whether this was intended or not, there can be little doubt that the church when constructed in this form suggested the idea of cruciform architecture, and so led on in much later times to the beautiful development of the Gothic churches of the North.

Orientation of Churches.

The innovation as to the altar had consequences which were no less momentous. Hitherto there had been a remarkable difference on the subject of the orientation of churches between Rome itself and the rest of Catholic Christendom. The Jewish practice of facing towards Jerusalem [1] at the time of prayer had passed into Christianity. When Jerusalem had been destroyed and the connection of the Christian Church with the city which had given it birth had consequently ceased to exist, churches were built facing the East, but with no relation to the actual direction of Jerusalem itself.[2] The altar was placed at the east end of the church, and priest and people alike faced to the East when the Holy Sacrifice was being offered. " All alike look to the East," is the direction in the " Didascalia ".[3]

This practice was apparently invariable throughout

---

[1] Cf. 1 Kings VIII. 38, 44 ; Dan. VI. 10 ; Ps. v. 7 ; Jonas II. 4.
[2] "Apost. Const.," ii., 57 ; Clem. Alex., "Strom.," vii., 7 ; Tert., "Apol.," 16.   [3] Ed. Funk, p. 124.

the whole world, with the solitary exception of the city of Rome, and those places where the influence of Rome was paramount. In Syria and in Egypt, in Africa, in Gaul and in Britain, we find the altar in the oldest churches placed at the east end of the Church. But in Rome, and under Roman influence, although the churches there also were built east and west, the altar was placed always at the western end and the church itself ran to the eastward. Whereas everywhere else priest and people faced in the same direction to the East when Mass was celebrated, in Rome the practice was different. The priest stood facing eastwards on the further side of the altar, looking down the church and facing the people who looked westwards towards him. This singular arrangement appears to be derived from the ritual directions contained in the Old Testament for the building of the Tabernacle[1] and of the Temple. Whereas in the rest of Christendom the arrangements of the church were apparently derived from the Synagogue, and the practice of all facing towards Jerusalem, or at least towards the East, thus came into being, the practice at Rome seems to have been deliberately based on the arrangements of the Temple itself, and the eastward position of the people at the time of prayer was consequently unknown. It is worth noting, perhaps, in this connexion that it is in the writings of St. Clement of Rome, and nowhere else in the Fathers before St. Cyprian, that the parallel of the Eucharistic sacrifice with its Jewish prototype is fully worked out.[2] It looks as if the doctrine had produced its logical result at Rome, and there alone, in the region of Church ceremonies.

The reversal of the orientation of St. Paul's had consequently a striking result so far as Roman

[1] Exod. xxvi., xxvii.
[2] Cf. Clem. Rom., I. iv., x. xxxi., xxxii., xxxvi., xl., xli., xliii., xliv.

14

Christianity was concerned. Now in that church, and nowhere else in the city, the celebrant stood as he did everywhere else with his back to the people and facing the apse in which was the bishop's throne. The consequence was that pilgrims to the Eternal City might see, possibly on consecutive days, the Pope saying Mass at St. Peter's facing eastwards down the church, and at St. Paul's still facing eastwards, but occupying the reverse position in relation to the church in which he was celebrating. So striking an object-lesson could not fail to impress men's minds, and the idea soon gained ground that the really important matter was the eastward position of the celebrant, and that so long as this was preserved it was of little consequence whether he faced down the church or towards the apse. The original idea of orientation, based upon the liturgical directions of the Tabernacle and Temple, passed out of view so far as the actual building was concerned, and the whole stress was henceforth laid upon the eastward position of the celebrant.

The next step in the development of our churches is illustrated by the earliest church at Canterbury; a conjectural plan of what it was before the fire of 1067 may be seen in Mr. G. G. Scott's "Essay on English Church Architecture". The arrangement still exists at the cathedrals of Maintz and Nauheim. A second altar, furnished with arrangements for a monastic choir, was placed in an apse at the eastern end of the church. There were now two high altars in the same church. The original one, at the western end of the church, was on the chord of the apse, and had the throne of the bishop immediately behind it. At this altar the celebrant faced eastwards down the church, as he had always done. At the other and newer altar (which in every instance known to us seems to have been a copy of the actual high altar at St. Peter's at

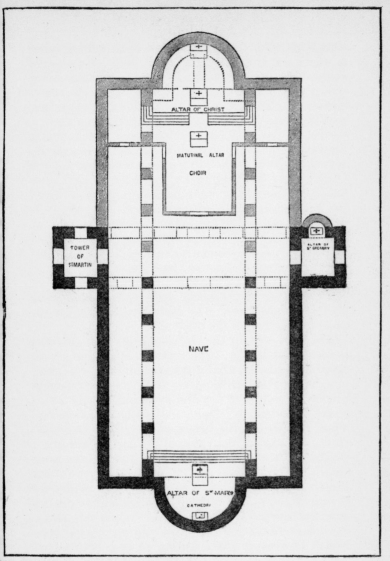

THE CATHEDRAL CHURCH OF CANTERBURY.   Conjectural plan by Mr. G. G. Scott. This shows the church as it was before the fire of A.D. 1067.   The black parts represent the original Basilica.

14 *

Rome, although its liturgical arrangement was that of St. Paul's and not of St. Peter's); the celebrant still faced eastwards but had his back to the main portion of the church. By degrees, owing perhaps in part to the greater frequency of the services at the monastic altar, the original altar being reserved for episcopal functions which were comparatively rare, the tendency grew up to regard the new altar, and not the original or episcopal altar, as the principal altar of the cathedral. Hence the lesser churches copied its arrangements for their own altars, and by degrees the original basilican arrangement died out of use, so that now it can hardly be met with outside of Rome itself.

The other innovation of the rebuilding of St. Paul's, the provision of the transverse nave, was soon found to be of great convenience, no doubt because of the greater room it allowed near the altar. Hence it seems speedily to have been adopted at the Lateran, where a similar enlargement was soon found to be necessary, and seems to have been carried out, as we have already said, by the Consul Flavius Felix, in the fifth century. At some later date the same thing was done at St. Peter's, but, as in the case of the Lateran, there is no specific mention in any record of the change. Our own belief, the reasons for which have been already given in another work,[1] is that it was not done until the very end of the Middle Ages, in 1470. While, on the one hand the tradition of the sixteenth century seems clear that a transverse nave did exist at the time of its destruction, it is remarkable that no early authority seems to speak of it, and that no one of the many pictorial representations which we possess depicts it as showing externally, though there is no difficulty at all about proving the existence of the one at St. Paul's. There

---

[1] " St. Peter in Rome," pp. 244 *seq.*, which see for details of the argument.

were great works of reparation carried out in 1470, and it is possible that the change was made then, and that the church from that time onwards imitated the arrangements of St. Paul's and the Lateran. There was, however, one important difference. The transverse nave at both the other two churches was beyond the altar, between it and the new apse. But at St. Peter's the new nave was made eastward of the apse and altar; a wholly different plan, but one which was much more in accordance with the ideas brought into being by the Gothic cruciform churches.

With the development of Gothic churches we have here no concern. In them the cruciform plan is carried much further, and the upper limb of the cross, which in the basilicas was only represented by the apse, becomes longer and longer in order to accommodate the choir. But to follow out these developments would carry us far beyond our present plan, and we must go back again to the earliest days after the peace of the Church in order to follow out the development of churches in the East, which took place on lines very different from those which obtained in the West.

Eastern Churches.

The origin of the Western Churches, we have contended, must be looked for in the Roman house, and the line of their development was fixed to the basilican type by the donation to the Church by Constantine of the Lateran Palace with its great private basilica. In the East the churches during the centuries of persecution were, no doubt, just as in the West, simply domestic houses of the locality put to this particular use. But the ordinary house in the East, whether in Egypt, in Syria, or in Asia Minor, was not constructed on the lines which Rome had taken over from Greece.

The essential difference lay in the plans for carrying the roof. In Greece and Rome the roof was carried by timbers, and was therefore sloping. In the East the roof of the house was flat, and was used as a terrace. As a rule the support was given by flat beams of stone, but in some structures the arch and dome were used. As, however, the skill arrived at in this form of construction was not as yet great, the unit of construction was necessarily small. Eastern buildings tended then, as to a great extent they do still, to be made up of a great number of small squares, each covered with a separate dome, which may or may not be manifested externally.

At first the basilican style had a very great vogue in the East as well as in the West. At Tyre the great church built by Constantine and described by Eusebius was a true basilica. At Jerusalem the church of the Anastasis and that of the Nativity at Bethlehem were also basilicas. In Egypt the White Monastery near Assiout survives to this day and is of the same type. At Constantinople the original church of Sta Sophia, built by Constantine, was a basilica, and so also was the original of SS. Sergius and Bacchus. The great mosque of Damascus seems to have been originally two basilican churches standing apse to apse which have now been united to form a single edifice of great beauty and striking proportions.

In spite of these magnificent examples the basilican style in the East was exotic and never really took root in the soil. Even Constantine himself seems to have felt this, for in his directions to Macarius of Jerusalem, quoted by Eusebius,[1] he expressly lays it down that either style of building (by which he means really either the timber beam form of construction for the roof or else the brick dome), might be employed in

---

[1] Eusebius, " Vita Constantini," iii. 32.

Palestine as was preferred. Almost from the first the
dome was the more frequent form of construction, and
the development of Byzantine architecture is accordingly along the lines thereby necessitated rather than
along those which were followed in the West. The
square church, surmounted by a circular dome, is the
type to which all conform, and from which all developments are ultimately derived.

In the country districts and where architecture was
not progressive, as in Egypt at this period, we find
churches built which in ground plan more or less
resemble the basilica. They have commonly three
haikals or sanctuaries, each square and with one side
built into an internal apse. But the number three
though usual in the North is very frequently exceeded
in the South. Several churches in Upper Egypt have
as many as seven haikals side by side.[1] These are
separated from the body of the church by screens, and
have each an altar in the centre, and seats round for
the clergy. The whole church is commonly roofed
by means of a number of small domes, each rising
from its own square unit, so that the resemblance to
the basilica does not go beyond the general ground
plan.

Such was the development in the country districts,
and churches built on this plan may be seen anywhere
in Egypt to-day. Size is obtained by the simple
method of putting a great number of square units side
by side, and in no other way. But at Constantinople
itself, where Greek architects were available and threw
themselves with enthusiasm into the conditions of the
problem, development was rapid. The adoption of
pendentives enabled the dome to be built of much

---

[1] Dr. Butler, " Coptic Churches," is wrong when he says the number of three is invariable. He had never been beyond Cairo and knew
nothing of Upper Egypt.

greater size without unduly increasing the thrust on the walls. From Constantinople the style spread to the West, and we get such interesting churches as those of S. Vitale at Ravenna and S. Lorenzo at Milan, both about the sixth century. All of them are square or nearly so, though this may be architecturally modified, so that they appear octagonal. All are roofed in by means of the dome, and belong, therefore, to the Eastern type rather than to the Western.

It was at Constantinople itself, however, that this Byzantine style reached its perfection. The original basilica of Sta Sophia, which had been built by Constantine, was burnt down about the year 530, and it was determined by Justinian the Emperor to rebuild it in the Byzantine style. The result was to produce a church which may fairly be called one of the wonders of the world. In it we have the element of the square unit with domed roof carried to its extreme development. It gives a finer central space than is possible with any other method, and at once became the model for the smaller churches of the East. Later on, when the architects of the West saw it at the time of the Crusades, and learnt from it what the possibilities of the dome really were, it influenced the production of St. Marco at Venice, and of the Gothic dome of the Cathedral of Florence. A little later it must be considered the parent of the great church of St. Peter's at Rome. After the capture of Constantinople by the Turks in 1453 it became the model for every great Turkish mosque. In our own day it has supplied the *motif* for the new Cathedral at Westminster, though this in turn has started a new development of its own just as St. Peter's did before it. No other church has ever had so much influence on later architecture as has been exercised by this great Cathedral of Sta Sophia at Constantinople.

Cruciform Architecture.

In the year 1216, or thereabouts, Pope Honorius III made another important change in one of the ancient basilicas. The Church of S. Lorenzo, as built by Constantine, was still standing, but it had long been far too small to accommodate the worshippers who came. A second basilica had, therefore, been built adjoining it end to end, but in the reverse direction, so that the two apses almost touched. Honorius determined to pull down the two apses, and then unite the churches, adding three more columns on each side. The later church then became the nave, and the older one the choir. The altar of the tomb, of course, remained the altar of the church in its new form. The floor of the earlier church was, however, much lower than that of the second basilica, because it had been dug out in order to get down to the actual tomb for the high altar. Honorius, therefore, inserted a new floor, supported on piers, at a level of about 3 feet higher than that of the new nave, and utilized the space underneath as a crypt. This new floor cuts across the lower columns at the side, which support the upper columns of the galleries, but the whole effect of the crypt and galleries is very fine.

The result of this innovation was that now there existed at Rome, in one of the great churches which every pilgrim went to visit, an arrangement which placed the high altar of the church in the centre, with the choir behind the altar, and the bishop's throne at the far end of this choir. Here, again, the development was almost accidental, but it was fertile in consequences. If it is to Sta Sophia that we must look for the revelation of the power of the dome to Western architects, it is to S. Lorenzo that the idea of placing the altar in the centre of the church is really due. There had been round churches at Rome before this. The baptistery constantly took this form ; and the Pantheon had been utilized for Christian worship, and the round church which enclosed the Holy Sepulchre had been frequently copied by the Templars on their return from Jerusalem. But in none of these churches had the altar been placed in the centre. It was always under one of the arches at the side of the building, and to place it in the centre would have seemed too bold a departure. But here at Rome, in one of the principal basilicas, the thing had been done, and a precedent existed. That precedent was made use of by the genius of Michael Angelo when he planned his new church of St. Peter's. His direct inspiration for the building came from pagan Rome, and not apparently, save indirectly, from any Christian building. What he said he would do was to take the dome of the Pantheon and place it above the basilica of Constantine. His original design was for a Greek cross, adding two more to the two half-domes which help to roof Sta Sophia, and making the church of a true cruciform shape. The necessity for providing room for great crowds, and also the desire to include in the new church every portion of the older building, led to the modifications, which he himself regretted, of the present ground plan. But here, again, we are far beyond our proper limits, and we must leave the subject of further developments to other hands. There is no more fascinating subject than the story of the developments of Gothic architecture and their relation to the needs of monastic and congregational worship, but it is a story which belongs to the Middle Ages, and lies outside the domain of Christian archæology. The archæologist has done his part when he has defined the conditions under which churches were originally built, and suggested the principal forces at work which are responsible for later developments and subsequent modifications.

BOOKS TO CONSULT.

1. *On the Whole Subject*—

Marucchi, *Éléments d'Archéologia Chrétienne.* 3 volumes. Rome, 1900-3.

Armellini, *Lezioni di archeologia cristiana.* Rome, 1898.

Leclercq, *Manuel d'Archéologie Chrétienne.* Paris, 1907.

Kraus, *Realescyklopädie der christlichen Alterthümer.* Freiburg, 1880-86.

Wilpert, *Principienfragen der christlichen Archäologie.* Freiburg, 1892.

Kaufmann, *Handbuch der christlichen Archäologie.* Paderborm, 1905.

De Rossi, *La Roma sotterranea cristiana.* Rome, 1864-77.

—— *Bullettino di archeologia cristiana.* Rome, 1863-94, 1896.

De Rossi and Others. *Nuovo Bullettino di arch. crist.* Rome, 1895-

Smith and Cheetham, *A Dictionary of Christian Antiquities.* London, 1876-80.

Martigny, *Dictionnaire des antiquités chrétiennes.* Paris, 1877.

Forrer, *Reallexicon der frühchristlichen Altertümer.* Berlin, 1907.

Cabrol, *Dictionnaire d'archéologie chrétienne et de liturgie.* Paris, 1902.

Naval, *Elementos de arqueologia.* S. Domingo, 1903.

De Rossi, *Inscriptiones Christianae urbis Romae VII° saeculo antiquiores.* Rome, 1861-88.

Northcote and Brownlow. *Roma Sotterranea.* London, 1869.

Marucchi, *I Monumenti del Museo Cristiano Pio-Lateranense.* Milan, 1910.

Sybel, L. von, *Christliche Antike.* Marburg, 1909.

2. *History of the First Three Centuries*—

Duchesne, *Liber Pontificalis.* Paris, 1886.

Allard, *Histoire des Persécutions.* Paris, 1885.

Grisar, *Storia di Roma e dei Papi.* Rome, 1899.

Krüger,. *Geschichte der altchristlichen Litteratur in der ersten drei Jahrhunderten.* Freiburg, 1895.

Ruinart, *Acta sincera Martyrum.* Paris, 1689.

Bollandists, *Acta Sanctorum.*

—— *Analecta Bollandiana.* Brussels, 1882.

Marucchi, *Le Memorie degli Apostoli Pietro e Paolo in Roma.*
  Rome, 1903.
Barnes, *St. Peter in Rome and his Tomb on the Vatican Hill.*
  London.
Lanciani, *Pagan and Christian Rome.* London, 1893.
Allard, *Ten Lectures on the Martyrs.* London, 1907.
—— *La Persécution de Diocletian et le triomphe de l'Église.* Paris,
  1903.
Doulcet, *Essai sur les rapports de l'Église chrétienne avec l'État
  Romain.* Paris, 1882.
Gregorovius, *History of the City of Rome in the Middle Ages.*
  London, 1902.

3. Early Christian Art—

Marchi, *I Monumenti delle arti cristiane nelle metropoli del
  cristianesimo.* Rome, 1844.
Garrucci, *Storia dell' arti cristiana.* Prato, 1873-
—— *Vetri ornati di figure in oro trovati nei cimeteri dei cristiani
  primitivi di Roma.* Roma, 1858.
Ghignoni, *El pensiero cristiano nell' arte.* Rome, 1903.
Millet, *La collection chrétienne et byzantine des Hautes-Études.*
  Paris, 1903.
Dalton, *Catalogue of early Christian antiquities of the British
  Museum.* London, 1901.
Lowrie, *Monuments of the Early Church.* New York, 1901.
Schultze, *Archäologie der Alt-christlichen Kunst.* Munich, 1895.
Wilpert, *Die Malereien der Katacombes Roms.* Freiburg, 1903.

4. Christian Epigraphy—

De Rossi, *Inscriptionis Christianae Urbis Romae VII° saeculo
  anteriores.* Rome, 1861-88.
Corpus inscriptionum graecarum. Berlin, 1828-77.
Corpus inscriptionum latinarum. Berlin, 1863.
Fabretti, *Inscriptionum antiquarum, etc.* Rome, 1699.
Hübner, *Inscriptiones Hispaniae christianae.* Berlin, 1871.
Kraus, *Inscriptiones rhenanae christianae.*
Le Blant, *Inscriptions chrétiennes de la Gaule.* Paris, 1856.
—— *Manuel d'epigraphie chrétienne.* Paris, 1869.
Marucchi, *Christian Epigraphy.* Cambridge, 1912.
Wilmanns, *Exempla inscriptionum latinarum.* Berlin, 1873.
Northcote, *Epitaphs of the Catacombs.* London, 1878.
McCall, *Christian Epitaphs of the First Six Centuries.* London,
  1869.

INDEX.

ABERDEEN: THE UNIVERSITY PRESS

THE
WESTMINSTER LIBRARY.

A SERIES OF MANUALS FOR CATHOLIC PRIESTS AND STUDENTS.

Edited by the Right Rev. Mgr. BERNARD WARD, President of St. Edmund's College, and the Rev. HERBERT THURSTON, S.J.

Crown 8vo. Price 3s. 6d. net each Volume.

THE TRADITION OF SCRIPTURE: its Origin, Authority, and Interpretation. By the Very Rev. WILLIAM CANON BARRY, D.D., sometime Scholar of the English College, Rome.

THE HOLY EUCHARIST. By the Right Rev. JOHN CUTHBERT HEDLEY, Bishop of Newport.

THE LEGENDS OF THE SAINTS: An Introduction to Hagiography. From the French of PÈRE H. DELEHAYE, S.J., Bollandist. Translated by Mrs. V. M. CRAWFORD.

THE PRIEST'S STUDIES. By the Very Rev. THOMAS SCANNELL, D.D., Canon of Southwark Cathedral, Editor of *The Catholic Dictionary*.

NON-CATHOLIC DENOMINATIONS. By the REV. ROBERT HUGH BENSON, M.A.

THE NEW PSALTER AND ITS USE. By the Rev. EDWIN BURTON, D.D., Vice-President of St. Edmund's College, Ware, and the Rev. EDWARD MYERS, M.A.

Crown 8vo. Price 5s. net.

THE EARLY CHURCH IN THE LIGHT OF THE MONUMENTS. By the Right Rev. Mgr. A. S. BARNES, M.A. With Illustrations.

Crown 8vo. Price 6s. net.

THE MASS: A Study of the Roman Liturgy. By ADRIAN FORTESCUE, D.D., D.Ph.

LONGMANS, GREEN AND CO., 39 Paternoster Row, London; New York, Bombay and Calcutta.